THE MARKETING MINUTE

A YEAR'S WORTH OF DAILY MARKETING IDEAS DESIGNED TO INSTIGATE AND INSPIRE

ALLEN HOWIE

PAPERBACK EDITION

ISBN: 978-0-9863340-1-6

This book is dedicated with enormous gratitude to my lovely wife, Lisa, who has been a constant source of love and encouragement; to my parents, Jim and Julie Howie, for helping me appreciate the value of hard work and perseverance; to my children, Emma, Sophie and Jack Howie, for a seemingly endless supply of comic relief; to the memory of Jim McCarthy, truest of friends; to David Kennedy, Andrew Burdsall and Duane Smith for deep wells of good counsel; and to God, the source of all big ideas.

CONTENTS

—

HOW TO USE THIS BOOK

The Marketing Minute began life about ten years ago as a (mostly) weekly e-mail to clients and friends. The goal was simple: to push ideas out into the world that might help marketing professionals and business owners find new ways to get their brands recognized and their messages heard in an increasingly noisy marketplace. My intention was to express those ideas succinctly enough that they could be read in a minute or less, and make them practical enough that they could be put into action.

This book collects some of the best of those ideas, and organizes them loosely by topic into four-week segments. It's designed so that it can be used as a sort of "devotional" for the reader looking for some daily marketing inspiration, or as a reference for someone who needs to focus on a specific area, such as building a brand or enhancing the service they provide. It includes space on each page for the reader / user to make notes about how that particular idea can be put into action, or what next steps might be required.

I hope you find it to be a practical tool and a reliable source of ideas as you work on refining your brand and marketing your company.

*"No one lights a lamp and then puts it under
a basket. Instead, a lamp is placed on a stand,
where it gives light to everyone in the house."*
Matthew 5:15

*"The best way to have a good idea is to have
lots of ideas."*
Linus Pauling

DAY ONE

Would you like to know how well your own people understand your brand? Try this test. Without preparing anyone ahead of time, have all of the key people in your organization (including yourself) write down a single sentence describing what makes you different from your competitors. Collect them all and compare notes. Strong brands elicit similar responses from insiders. If most of the descriptions are similar, you probably have a strong internal sense of your brand. If not, you have some work to do.

ACTION: *If you need to strengthen the internal perception of your brand, what are three things you could do to help your team truly internalize what makes you different? Which one could you do this week?*

_____

_____

_____

_____

_____

_____

_____

_____

DAY TWO

Remember that task from the previous page: writing a single descriptive sentence that clearly tells how you're a better choice than your competitors? Let's add a degree of difficulty. Don't use any of the following words: quality, service, expertise, excellent, selection or value. Can you still do it? The problem with all those "generic" descriptive words is that they're not so descriptive after all. Your competitors would almost certainly use them to describe themselves. Once you get away from those words that have lost their meaning through overuse, you'll force yourself to use words that get to the heart of your brand.

ACTION: *Write a single statement defining your brand — why it's different from and better than your competitors — that doesn't use any "generic" terms.*

_____

_____

_____

_____

_____

_____

_____

DAY THREE

A great tagline distills your brand essence into one memorable statement. See if you know these companies or products by their taglines. "When it absolutely, positively has to be there overnight." "The quicker picker-upper." "Takes a licking and keeps on ticking." "The nighttime, sniffling, sneezing, coughing, aching, stuffy head, fever so you can rest medicine." "It's everywhere you want to be." All of these examples clearly define the brand position in a memorable way — and none of them could be adopted by a competitor. If you have a tagline, does it clarify your brand position? And if you don't have a tagline…why not?

(**Answers**: Federal Express, Bounty, Timex, Vicks Nyquil, Visa)

ACTION: *Try to craft a short, powerful tagline that clarifies what you do and how you do it differently / better.*

_____

_____

_____

_____

_____

_____

_____

DAY FOUR

Bob Fosse, who directed "Cabaret" and whose choreography helped make "Chicago" a sultry surprise hit, was known among his dancing peers for having bad feet, poor posture and limited flexibility. But Fosse turned those very "deficiencies" to his advantage, creating a style of dance built on very sharp, isolated movements. As a result, he's one of the two or three choreographers Americans can actually name, and probably the only one with a movie (*All That Jazz*) based on his career. The lesson for your company? If circumstances prevent you from operating in the same way as your competitors, look for ways to turn those limitations into advantages. That's how you become a vital brand.

ACTION: *What limitations or circumstances keep you from doing what your competition does? Brainstorm ways to turn those "limitations" into a better, smarter way to compete.*

_____

_____

_____

_____

_____

_____

_____

DAY FIVE

Businesses often watch what their competitors do, then try to emulate them, pulling elements from various sources to create a new, if unremarkable, whole. There are entire consulting practices based on gathering successful businesses together to share and replicate their marketing approaches. This is the polar opposite of branding. While there's value in understanding what's working for other, similar businesses, it's all moving too fast today, and you can't build a brand, gain market share or boost traffic simply by doing what the other guy does. You have to become the one they're chasing. Be the company that's ahead of the pack, trying new approaches, getting closer to customers and exploring new, more effective marketing channels.

ACTION: *What are two ways you follow the competition? How can you stop? What are two things you could begin doing now to pull away from the pack?*

_____

_____

_____

_____

_____

_____

_____

DAY ONE

Jack Trout is the co-author of *Positioning*, one of the most important marketing and branding books ever written. In a more recent work, *A Genie's Wisdom*, he warns of the danger of placing growth above your mission. If growth is the goal, he cautions, then a business will do whatever it takes to grow, adding products or services that have little or no connection to its mission. In this "something for everyone" process, it often gives away the unique position which gave it momentum in the first place. Instead, Trout suggests, focus on deepening your particular niche and fulfilling your mission. Do that well, and growth always follows.

ACTION: *What is the "sweet spot" for your brand — the specific products or services you deliver best? Instead of adding new ones at which you don't excel, how can you enhance or add value to those at which you shine the brightest?*

_____

_____

_____

_____

_____

_____

DAY TWO

Instead of being a mediocre magician (which he was), Harry Houdini decided to become something new - an escape artist. No one would have guessed that audiences would sit for ninety minutes or more while someone they couldn't see tried to get out of a box. But they did, and Harry became more famous than any magician of his day. Likewise, Cirque du Soleil, which began as a group of street performers, reinvented the circus, ditching the animals and amping up the theatricality. Today, their brand is as recognized worldwide as Disney and McDonald's. Is it possible to rethink what you do in such a way that you create a whole new ballgame?

ACTION: *If you had to take the basic elements of what you do and recast your company as a completely different kind of entity, what would it be?*

_____

_____

_____

_____

_____

_____

_____

_____

DAY THREE

Brand-building is a time-honored discipline. A century before celebrity endorsements and naming rights for performance venues became commonplace, they were already being used by piano maker Steinway & Sons. Steinway Hall in New York housed the New York Philharmonic for a quarter of a century. And while everyone from Franz Liszt to Cole Porter performed only on Steinways, the company never paid any of its celebrity endorsers. Noted schools like Julliard only use Steinways, and over 1,300 musicians are "Steinway Artists," a distinction earned by both owning one of the famed pianos and using them exclusively in performances. Not bad branding for a 150-year-old company.

ACTION: *Even within a smaller market, can your company become the "provider of choice" for the most prestigious customers? How could you start?*

_____

_____

_____

_____

_____

_____

DAY FOUR

When Virgin Atlantic Airways was launched, an established competitor scoffed, "What does Richard Branson know about the airline business? He comes from the entertainment business." Over 20 years later, Virgin is far more profitable than that competitor. Likewise, Danny Meyers, who owns 4 of the 20 top-rated restaurants in New York City, pointed out in a recent interview, "We're in the business of delivering an experience that's supposed to make you feel good." Because both Branson and Meyers focus on hospitality as their core business, they've created customer magnets.

ACTION: *What business are you really in? How could a shift in focus to that business change the way you do everything?*

_____

_____

_____

_____

_____

_____

_____

_____

DAY FIVE

Who do you love? Think of your favorite business - a place you look forward to visiting. It could be a restaurant, a bookstore, a coffee shop, a clothing store, a spa, a fitness center — any kind of business. Why is it your favorite? What makes you look forward to going there? Chances are that there are very specific qualities you associate with that destination that make you anticipate your next visit. Together, those qualities combine to create a singular brand experience for you. How can your company become your customers' favorite place?

ACTION: *Write down everything you love about your favorite places to do business of any kind. Can any or all of those qualities transfer to your business?*

_____

_____

_____

_____

_____

_____

_____

_____

DAY ONE

Like it or not, we all think in stereotypes. If someone's introduced as an accountant, an actor or a pharmaceutical sales rep, our brains immediately plug those people into preassigned roles before we know them as people at all. Prospects do the same with businesses. So as you work on your brand, take a big step backwards and ask two questions. What do people think of your industry? What do they think of people who work in your industry? The answers to those two questions will give you some sense of the true challenges you face as you try to carve out a niche for yourself.

ACTION: *How can you use what people think of your industry and your people to your advantage? Can you turn a stereotype on its head?*

DAY TWO

In the wake of a pet food contamination story, producers of natural pet food made from locally grown ingredients enjoyed astronomic growth — even though their products cost much more. Likewise, when the housing market was struggling, the problems in the mortgage market spurred a small return to banks and away from more transient mortgage brokers or lenders. Unfortunately, you can't depend on a crisis to appear and boost your business. What could banks or pet food companies have done before now to accomplish the same thing?

ACTION: *If you enjoy a singular advantage over your competitors – an advantage that would become more critical if a problem arose among those competitors – how can you use that advantage to drive sales now?*

_____

_____

_____

_____

_____

_____

_____

DAY THREE

Not sure that owning a "brand" is all that valuable? Consider this. Every major supermarket sells "store brands" - generic versions of the branded products on its shelves. Every consumer knows that the same companies that make the "branded" product often make the store brands. So if customers know that a store brand is the same quality as the well-known name, at a fraction of the cost, store brands must outsell their more expensive counterparts, right? Not even close. Store brands and generics account for only about 7% of total sales. That's the value of a brand — the preferred choice can charge a premium price. Brand matters.

ACTION: *Don't just consider your own brand vs. others. Among your own products or services, can you create premium brands that become the preferred choice? What's your first step?*

DAY FOUR

Time and again, attaching positive emotions to a brand gives that brand traction. Think of everyone from Jell-O (the old Bill Cosby spots) to Nike. Schwinn did the same for its brand with a smart campaign that positioned riding a Schwinn as the antidote to all the technological barriers standing between us and the simpler pleasures of life. Check it out along with other Schwinn videos online, and see if it doesn't make you want to take a ride.

ACTION: *What emotional benefit do your products or services provide? How can you tap into that emotion with your marketing?*

_____

_____

_____

_____

_____

_____

_____

_____

DAY FIVE

Most people who were around in the 1980s remember the New Coke fiasco. What you may not recall is why it happened. Pepsi was gaining ground with its "Pepsi Challenge" blind taste tests. So Coke worked on a new formula until it found one that beat Pepsi in taste tests, then launched it as New Coke. The rest is history — as is New Coke. Coca-Cola let itself be drawn into playing Pepsi's game, rather than creating an innovative marketing program of its own.

ACTION: *Do you lead the competition or follow it? The strongest brands create their own marketing game, then play it better than anyone else. Do you?*

_____

_____

_____

_____

_____

_____

_____

_____

_____

DAY ONE

If your brand could use a role model, try the United States Marine Corps. A recent advertising campaign focused on how only the toughest and best become Marines. Shot at Parris Island by a director who helped direct the Normandy Beach footage for *Saving Private Ryan*, it shows real Marines enduring all the rigors of basic training - including vomiting from tear gas, plunging into a pool in full uniform and taking a blow to the head during combat training. Long ago, the Marines decided to build their brand not by making it seem more glamorous, but by positioning themselves as the most demanding and rigorous of America's fighting forces.

ACTION: *Is there a way to apply this approach to your own recruiting efforts? Could you even apply it to your customer marketing?*

_____

_____

_____

_____

_____

_____

_____

_____

DAY TWO

A study revealed that during the last recession, the brands which remained strongest did so because they were among the most trusted. The brands which fared worst were often those who lost the trust of consumers - especially those in the financial sector. This suggests that a primary goal of your ongoing marketing and public relations efforts should be to build trust among existing and potential customers.

ACTION: *What level of trust do your company and your industry enjoy among your best potential customers? What should you do about that right now?*

_____

_____

_____

_____

_____

_____

_____

_____

_____

_____

DAY THREE

When people were asked recently what they valued at work, job security outperformed high pay two to one. Because your people are a key (maybe *the* key) driver of your brand, why not tie job security to brand building? Those employees (from the mail room to the boardroom) who live the brand and demonstrate the company's values every day should know with certainty that they have the most secure positions. Those who seem indifferent or erode the brand's value through their performance should understand that their positions are in peril.

ACTION: *Who among your team is actively building your brand? Are they rewarded for it? Who's undermining it? Why are they still with you?*

_____

_____

_____

_____

_____

_____

_____

_____

DAY FOUR

Here's a question every business owner, manager or marketing director should ask from time to time: Would you be a customer of your own company? Given everything that you know, and all the choices you have, would you choose you? Be honest. If you would, why would you? Therein lies your brand statement. If you wouldn't, why not? The answer to *that* question is the start of your to-do list.

ACTION: *How can you take this question to key team members today and turn their responses into either a brand statement or a punch list?*

DAY FIVE

Of all the tactics you can employ to make your marketing work harder, probably none has more potential to boost your sales than genuine empathy — being able to put yourself in someone else's position. When your sales pitch, your marketing message or the flow of your website demonstrates a real understanding of the prospect's needs and desires, challenges and obstacles, you open the door for that person to have a relationship with your business and your brand. And brand loyalty is built on exactly such relationships.

ACTION: *How can your brand demonstrate a little empathy toward those you're courting today? Can you identify three ways you can do this better now?*

DAY ONE

During a recent move, a small, local bedding manufacturer and retailer, Bowles Mattress Company, actually talked a customer *out* of buying a new mattress and springs, noting that the customer's existing set still had plenty of life left in it. A lost sale today? Yes. A customer for life? You bet. And the lifetime value of a customer is often measured in thousands of dollars. Sometimes the best way to gain a customer is lose a sale, if the product or service isn't right for that customer at that time. It's a reminder that sales is about helping customers or clients get what they really need and avoid what they don't.

ACTION: *Do your salespeople have the option of talking a customer out of a purchase if that purchase isn't the right fit for them? Do they know that? What do you need to do to drive that point home?*

_____

_____

_____

_____

_____

_____

_____

DAY TWO

A recent study of shoppers revealed a number of insights that can help you sell more. For example, nearly a third of all shoppers make impulse purchases once they're in a store. And almost 40% don't make their brand decisions until they're in the store, with those choices swayed most often by product demonstrations. If your customers visit you in person, this is critical to increasing your sales.

ACTION: *How should this affect what customers see in your store? And if you're a service provider, how can you use this information to sell more services?*

DAY THREE

The fastest way to become known as a wonderful conversationalist is to get people to relax and talk about themselves and their interests. You may end up saying very little, but they'll remember that they had a lovely conversation with you. This is vital in sales. Most salespeople spend far too much time worrying about their "pitch." Everyone practices their "elevator speech" - summing up what they do in the time it takes an elevator between stops. But the truth is, listening is far more important in the sales process than talking. Learn to ask questions that lead a prospect to see for themselves the need for what you do, and let them invite you to solve their problems. It may sound counter-intuitive, but gifted salespeople all understand this idea perfectly.

ACTION: *How good are you or your sales team at listening? What training do they need to ask questions that encourage the prospect to do the talking?*

_____

_____

_____

_____

_____

_____

_____

DAY FOUR

Businesses often use a "hook" to get first-time buyers in the door - an introductory offer, a free sample, a coupon — even free luggage. But what happens next is often neglected. No one sets the hook. You have an opportunity to show the new buyer why you're different — to create an experience that demonstrates what a great choice they've made. In short, you have the chance to turn them into loyal customers. But too often, we expend all our energy baiting the hook, and precious little on reeling in the catch. Then we're surprised when so many of the big ones get away.

ACTION: *Does your marketing plan include strategies and training designed to convert your hard-won prospects into loyal customers? If not, how can you start?*

_____

_____

_____

_____

_____

_____

_____

_____

DAY FIVE

Spring is the time of year when newly-minted college graduates start their job searches. But often, probably in an effort to just get a foot in the door, they introduce themselves in a very vague way, looking for "any openings you may have." Such a request is easy to ignore, because that's all it is — one request among many. Salespeople do this with prospects, too. "Do you have any financial / health / other needs we can meet?" Like a new grad, your company should know where you want to be, and show the prospect how you can help them in a very specific way, with expertise and experience only you can offer.

ACTION: *How can you help your salespeople transition from vague inquiries to guided, brand-focused questions?*

_____

_____

_____

_____

_____

_____

_____

DAY ONE

If you're in sales, or have salespeople, the law of averages says you'll hear "no" more often than "yes." Sales is not a profession for the faint of heart. But think about the person who has to tell you "no." With a few loutish exceptions, no one likes to turn another person down. It's hard and can be awkward. So you score a lot of points with the prospect if you accept every "no" gracefully, express gratitude for the time the prospect invested and the opportunity you were given, and ease the tension of the moment. They'll remember that you responded with maturity and made the experience a little easier for them. And that means you'll stay on their list and in their good graces when the next opportunity rolls around. Gracious losers win more in the long run.

ACTION: *Do you or your sales team handle "no" graciously? How can you put a process in place to turn that "no" into the start of a relationship — by adding the prospect to an e-mail list, scheduling a date to revisit their needs, etc?*

_____

_____

_____

_____

_____

_____

DAY TWO

If there's one problem that stumps most salespeople, it's how to clearly communicate what makes them different from their competitors. Here's one way. If you treat clients better than anyone else, start treating prospects as if they were clients. If you send out special invitations to clients, send them to your best prospects as well. If your clients get timely reminders and recommendations from you, make sure prospects get them, too. If you have client events, invite prospects. Let the person or business you want for a client see firsthand how well you'll serve them. Do it right, and they won't be a prospect for long - they'll become a client.

ACTION: *What are three things you can do to treat clients like prospects? What has to happen to put one of those three things in place right away?*

_____

_____

_____

_____

_____

_____

_____

DAY THREE

Fifth Third Bank launched a campaign targeting high school and college students and their parents, designed to help young people learn to handle money well before they develop bad habits. The marketing effort uses humor to warn students about being "that guy" who's always hitting his friends up for a little cash and leaves college with huge credit card bills. The campaign includes educational material and programs along with more traditional marketing messages, and has been well-received.

ACTION: *Can you educate prospects in a way that helps them become better users of your products or services? What do you need to begin?*

DAY FOUR

Marketing guru Theodore Levitt famously noted, "People don't want to buy a quarter-inch drill. They want a quarter-inch hole." His point is that too many businesses forget to sell the benefit of their product or service. How can you tell if you're one of them? Your website and brochures have lots of bullet-point lists of things you offer. The copy never includes the word "you." It never poses a question for which your product or service is the answer. It's a timeless rule that bears repeating: stop selling features, and get back to selling benefits. If you can't make someone's life better, no one is interested.

ACTION: *Look at your website, your collateral and your sales training material. Do they focus on the benefits you offer and the problems you solve — and on how you do both differently from your competitors?*

_____

_____

_____

_____

_____

_____

_____

_____

SELL | WEEK TWO

DAY FIVE

"Product" is one of the old "Five P's" of marketing (along with price, place, people and promotion), meaning that *what* you choose to sell is a marketing decision as important as how you promote it. Yet many marketing decisions are made not on the basis of what consumers want, but on the basis of what the company needs to sell. As odd as it seems, it takes guts to stop selling the thing no one really wants, and switch to selling what's really in demand. But it's the only way to succeed.

ACTION: *Are you selling what your customers want today? How do you know? What opportunities are you missing?*

---

42   THE MARKETING MINUTE

DAY ONE

We've had light bulbs for well over a century. So how is it that candles are still around? In fact, how is it that there are whole stores devoted to selling candles, and that the industry generates over $2 billion a year? It's a great example of two ideas. First, if you can find new uses for old technology, you can make a lot of money. Second, if you can focus on the emotional rather than the practical (people don't buy candles for practical reasons), you can sell more.

ACTION: *Can you identify a new reason for people to use what you offer — even something you used to offer that became irrelevant? What are the emotional reasons people buy from you? How can you focus on those?*

DAY TWO

In sales, there's a mistaken notion that staying in front of the prospect is always a good thing. It isn't. Pointless contact with prospects (or even customers), simply for the sake of the contact itself, wastes their valuable time. Likewise, dropping in to show them something you have to sell is a time waster. But showing up with a solution or an idea - something that can help their company grow — now *that's* worth a visit. If you or your sales team can eliminate "drive-by sales" and invest your time in genuinely helping your clients, you'll have all the business you need.

ACTION: *Take time to sit down with your prospect list and come up with at least one solid suggestion or idea you can offer each one. Then think of the best way to present each one. How many new clients would make this effort worthwhile?*

_____

_____

_____

_____

_____

_____

_____

_____

DAY THREE

Too many salespeople believe that their goal is to persuade you to buy. This sets up an almost instant adversarial relationship. You push, the prospect resists. Even the language we use — "overcoming objections" — suggests overpowering the prospect. The best salespeople know that their job is to first find those prospects for whom your product or service is a good fit, then present it to them that way. When what you do is the solution to a problem or makes life easier — when it's a good fit — it "sells" itself.

ACTION: *How do you or your salespeople know when a prospect is a good fit for what you sell? Can you develop a system to help find the best matches?*

_____

_____

_____

_____

_____

_____

_____

_____

_____

_____

DAY FOUR

We tend to think that great salespeople are successful because they're likable folks who speak well and persuasively. But while those traits matter, the consensus seems to be that persistence marks the cream of the crop. Great salespeople start with a great product or service, find people who would genuinely be better off with that product or service, then stay in front of them for the duration. Business books are crammed with success stories based almost entirely on simply outworking and outlasting the competition. And it's not just salespeople - persistent marketing outperforms erratic or inconsistent efforts every time.

ACTION: *How can you measure the persistence of your team? How can you identify persistence when you hire sales people? Is persistence part of your sales training?*

_____

_____

_____

_____

_____

_____

_____

DAY FIVE

Success in any endeavor is great. Among its benefits, it provides positive reinforcement for those who achieve it. But there's a downside - and potentially a big one. All that reinforcement makes it very hard for successful people to change. And if there's one constant in sales and marketing today, it's change. If you manage salespeople — or if you are one — overcoming this success-driven resistance to change is the key to future success.

ACTION: *Try this: identify one sales practice in your company that's less fruitful than it used to be, then ask yourself what change might overcome those diminishing returns. How can you implement that change today?*

DAY ONE

In this economy, if you're asking consumers or other businesses to write a big check, your pitch better be a bold one. A timid or tepid request for a customer's business, especially for big ticket items, is likely to be met with indifference. If you want to persuade someone to act in a big way, you have to ask in a big way. Consider the Marines. Enlistment ought to be a tough sell right now, with so much unrest in the world. But marketing for the Corps has only gotten tougher, stressing the brutal demands placed on anyone who wants to join. The result? They continue to exceed their recruiting goals.

ACTION: *If you're asking prospects to take a big step, brainstorm bold ways to present the benefits to them.*

DAY TWO

It's amazing how many business-to-business sales appeals simply present what's available, then ask if there's interest. No offer of a true benefit to the prospect. No solution to the prospect's problem. No value added over similar products or services. Just, "Here it is - want it?" Worse yet is a sales pitch that focuses on what the seller needs (meet a deadline, fill a quota, etc.) and ignores what the prospect needs. If you can't help a client make money, or save time or money, or add value in some other way that truly matters, your sales pitch will nearly always fall on deaf ears.

ACTION: *Does your sales presentation focus unwaveringly on what the client needs first? Does your solution meet that need in a unique, valuable way? If not, what changes need to happen to your product or your pitch?*

DAY THREE

A lot of businesses face the same challenge - how to get customers to change behaviors. Think of a gym, a weight loss program, a credit counselor, a tutoring service or even a doctor. If your company relies on customers making tough lifestyle changes, remember the importance of short-term wins. For example, credit counseling companies often encourage customers to pay off their smallest loan or credit card balance first. That accomplishes two things. It gives the customer a sense of real progress, which motivates them to continue. And it frees up resources to apply to the next loan, so progress accelerates.

ACTION: *How can you inspire change over the long haul, and find ways to celebrate short-term gains with your customers?*

_____

_____

_____

_____

_____

_____

_____

DAY FOUR

Two events in the not-so-distant past point to the importance of knowing what matters. First, Gidget, the chihuahua made famous by those Taco Bell commercials, passed away. The most memorable thing about Gidget for marketers was not her popularity, but the fact that the very popular campaign barely nudged the sales needle for the restaurants. On the other hand, industry experts predicted disaster for KFC's foray into grilled chicken. Results suggest what, according to CEO David Novak, may be the most successful product launch in the chain's history. As both stories show, at the end of the day, sales are the only marketing metric that matter.

ACTION: *How do you measure the success of your sales and marketing efforts? How do you use those metrics to change what you're doing?*

DAY FIVE

There are plenty of salespeople out there calling on your prospects. They're calling on your customers, too. It would be depressing except for one fact - so many of them do it so badly. Just seconds into most sales calls, it becomes clear that the salesperson wants to tell you everything except how he or she can help your business. Oh, they'll tell you what products or services they offer. But while they have lots of ways you can add to their bottom line, they rarely bring you an idea that can boost yours. If you have salespeople - or if you are one - be the exception.

ACTION: *How does your sales approach compare with your competitors? Is yours focused on the prospect's business instead of yours? Do your sales materials reflect this, too?*

_____

_____

_____

_____

_____

_____

_____

DAY ONE

In Hamlet's last soliloquy, Shakespeare uses the phrase, "Damn with faint praise." It's a good reminder that you can undermine your own marketing efforts by using tired or tepid words. At a recent event where people were given two minutes to pitch their businesses, at least two used the word "decent" to describe their company's abilities. Lackluster words like these, as well as shopworn phrases like "personal service," "competitive pricing" and "high quality," actually undermine your brand by making you sound generic. Like the Bard himself, choose your words carefully.

ACTION: *Take a good look at everything from your website to your marketing materials and sales presentations. How many overused, tired and meaningless words and phrases can you find? With what dynamic word or phrase could you replace each?*

_____

_____

_____

_____

_____

_____

_____

DAY TWO

To prove a point about the value of creative advertising, some ad agency folks bought a used BMX bike on eBay, re-listed it using amped up copy ("wicked sick BMX") and sold that same bike for five times what they paid for it. The upshot? Copy counts. Whether it's your website, a brochure, a direct mail piece or a radio spot, does your copy sound like everyone else's?

ACTION: *How can you rewrite your advertisements to be more dynamic and — dare we say it — fun to read? You might be surprised at the impact on your sales.*

_____

_____

_____

_____

_____

_____

_____

_____

_____

DAY THREE

Here's an actual Facebook message we received. "Saw a bank billboard today with the words 'Your Money Matters To Us' on it. Now, first, that's just wrong thinking to me. Your DREAMS matter to us; Your HOME matters; Your SUCCESS matters to us, etc...right? Not a cold 'your MONEY matters'! To top it off, it had the standard collection of 3 executives looking trustworthy and next to them...wait for it...YUP - A DOG!! WHAAAAAAAAT??????????" This is lazy marketing - and a great example of how quickly consumers see through such poorly-conceived, self-serving messages. Consumers don't care what matters to you - unless it's them. To quote Rick Warren out of context, "It's not about you." Worst of all, the billboard in question was for a *new* bank. How do you think they'll do?

ACTION: *Who is the focus of your marketing — you or your prospects? Is it believable / authentic / original? If not, how can you make it so?*

_____

_____

_____

_____

_____

_____

DAY FOUR

"You do not get," the scripture declares, "because you do not ask." So try this. Look at everything that constitutes your marketing — website, brochure, advertising, social media presence, etc. Does each one ask the prospect to do something? Not enable them — *ask* them? If not, why not? Isn't that what you want? If you know you should ask for the business when you meet with a new prospect, why wouldn't you require the same of your marketing tools? In every instance where you touch the customer, always include a call to action. Say what you'd like them to do, then ask them to do it.

ACTION: *Do an inventory of every marketing message you have out there — print, broadcast and digital. Does each ask for the business or include a clear call to action?*

_____

_____

_____

_____

_____

_____

_____

DAY FIVE

Of all the marketing decisions that get made every day, perhaps none is more arbitrary than color. The vast majority of the time, color choices (for logos, for brochures, for websites) are made not on the basis of established color theory, but on personal preference by the decision-maker. Even though we know that certain colors and palettes evoke specific responses, colors are rarely chosen on that basis. Personal preferences can undermine the effectiveness of marketing if the color or colors selected are at odds with the brand message and the reaction you hope to create in the consumer. It may seem like a small thing, but when it comes to building or breaking your brand, the small things matter.

ACTION: *From your logo and marketing materials to your website and even customer contact areas of your business, are color choices appropriate for what you do and who you serve. Or are they based on personal taste?*

DAY ONE

Often, the conventional way of doing things is so ingrained that it becomes impossible to see it objectively anymore. You've probably seen a banner outside a medical practice - doctor, dentist, etc. - that reads, "Now Accepting New Patients." What message does this send? If the message is "New patients welcome here" or "We love new patients" or "New patients love it here," does it change what you think about that practice?

ACTION: *Look at your own marketing. Are you accepting or embracing new customers, allowing them in or welcoming them? What one thing could you change to make your message - and your brand - more inviting?*

_____

_____

_____

_____

_____

_____

_____

_____

_____

DAY TWO

Imagine you want a girl to go to the prom with you. You stand by her in the hall. You talk about your car, your dancing skills, your tux, how nice she looks…but never actually say the words, "Be my date for the prom." Even if she *wanted* to be your date, she eventually loses interest and wanders away. That's what happens with most marketing. It talks up the company, but never asks the prospect to do anything specific…so they wander off and find another date. If you want results, ask for the business. "Lose 10 pounds by Memorial Day." "Open an Account and Save $10 Instantly."

ACTION: *What do you want prospects to do? Have you told them?*

_____

_____

_____

_____

_____

_____

_____

_____

_____

DAY THREE

In a price-sensitive world, there's always a temptation to grow profits by cutting costs. But what about increasing your prices? In any economy, people will always pay more for certain attributes. People pay more for speed, for convenience, for "green" alternatives, for new technology, for flexibility, for home delivery, for the chance to help a cause, for cool design and much more. If you're in a business where profit margins have tightened, consider all the reasons people are willing to pay a little extra, and adjust your offerings accordingly.

ACTION: *Brainstorm a list of everything people will pay more to get. Compare that list to what you offer. Which can you incorporate that would let you ask — and get — higher prices for what you do?*

_____

_____

_____

_____

_____

_____

_____

_____

DAY FOUR

The annual post-game conversation about which Super Bowl spots were most memorable begs a much larger question. Why not look at every one of your marketing messages as if the Super Bowl was your stage? Every TV commercial. Every radio spot. Every billboard. Every social media promotion. Every ad in print. Successful Super Bowl spots may have big budgets, but what makes them memorable are the ideas that drive them — and great ideas scale down to even the smallest business. If you knew that your next message would be seen by millions, would it change your message — and its execution?

ACTION: *Imagine your next marketing message (regardless of media) was going to appear on the Super Bowl broadcast. What would you do differently?*

_____

_____

_____

_____

_____

_____

_____

_____

DAY FIVE

Why is Zappo's so popular? You might talk about the deep selection offered by the online shoe retailer, or guess that it's pricing that makes them prosper. But the truth is probably much simpler. With free shipping and free returns for a year, Zappo's removed the argument for not buying from them. Then selection and price did the rest.

ACTION: *What argument can you remove from the buying decision by changing your processes?*

_____

_____

_____

_____

_____

_____

_____

_____

_____

DAY ONE

With all the focus on using social media to display your expertise, it's easy to overlook the impact of a real, live seminar, workshop or demonstration where presenter and attendees interact in the moment and the expertise has to be real and deep. Why do people still attend concerts, plays and ballgames when they can see it all on screens? The experience can feel much richer and more valuable when you're there, in the moment.

ACTION: *Looking ahead, what can you share with clients and prospects that they would value enough to show up in person? List some ideas, then grab a calendar and set some dates.*

_____

_____

_____

_____

_____

_____

_____

_____

_____

_____

DAY TWO

It's safe to say that at least 95% of all marketing messages go relatively unnoticed…and for one simple reason. They don't command attention. Regardless of the medium, effective marketing makes you stop and look or listen. It distracts you from everything else. Then, it does one more thing: it sets the hook. It gives you something that makes you feel the distraction was worth it. It plants a seed or inflames a desire, in a way that lasts after the message is over.

ACTION: *Is your marketing in the most profitable 5%? If not, what needs to happen to put it there? How can your message stop traffic?*

_____

_____

_____

_____

_____

_____

_____

_____

DAY THREE

Let's be frank. Unless you are wired very differently than most people, there's nothing sexy about a tote bag, sparkly or otherwise. But calling it sexy is smart. Especially when you're Victoria's Secret, and sexy is what you sell. It's like adding "Brazilian" in front of…well, almost anything. What Victoria's Secret knows, and what more marketers should practice, is that words matter. Dressing your product or service up with words like sexy or smart draws in the audience for whom those qualities are aspirational. So no matter what you sell, add a little sparkle. It can't hurt.

ACTION: *What aspirational qualities can you assign to the products or services you're selling? Then how can you incorporate those into your marketing? Make it sparkle.*

_____

_____

_____

_____

_____

_____

_____

DAY FOUR

Imagine yourself back in school. Your assignment: come up with an idea for a really interesting story about your company. A story so appealing that almost anyone would want to hear it. Here's why that make-believe assignment matters. As newspapers shrink and television news leans more heavily on the sensational than ever before, your opportunities to get meaningful coverage in traditional media are dwindling. That means you have to work harder than ever before to get the attention of stressed-out, overworked assignment editors and reporters.

ACTION: *What's your story? If you don't have one, how can you create one?*

DAY FIVE

Research shows that consumers of every age appreciate "loyalty rewards," special offers from the brands they frequent. But they prefer to hear about them in different ways. More than ever before, seniors are reading the statements, special offers and surveys they receive in the mail from companies they do business with. At the other end of the spectrum, millennials prefer mobile calls, text messages and contact via social media sites. If you have a rewards program - or are considering one - take into account the best ways to get a response from different kinds of customers.

ACTION: *First question: do you have a loyalty rewards program of some kind? If not, why not — especially if it isn't traditionally done in your industry. Now — how will you stay in touch with those loyal users in a way that works for each?*

_____

_____

_____

_____

_____

_____

_____

DAY ONE

Many years ago, advertising legend David Ogilvy wrote, "If you're trying to persuade people to do something, or buy something, it seems to me you should use their language, the language they use every day, and the language in which they think." While researchers have confirmed the wisdom of this strategy over and over again, it's amazing how many companies convey their marketing messages in stiff, lifeless prose, wielding language no one ever uses when talking about that same product or service. The result? Brochures, ads, e-mails and web pages that never get read. Copy is supposed to sell. If you want to sell, write the way people speak.

ACTION: *Take a look over your brochures, ads, e-mails and website. Are they easy and enjoyable for your customer to read? If not, what changes do you need to make?*

_____

_____

_____

_____

_____

_____

_____

DAY TWO

Sometimes it makes sense to state the obvious. So here goes. You want customers to do business with you. Customers could not care less. This is the point where marketing begins. You have to do two things. Get the prospect's attention. Then give them a great reason to do whatever you want them to do. The first part absolutely requires creativity - a unique way of getting the audience to look or listen. The second part requires creativity, too — finding or creating something truly unique about the way you serve customers. No one cares about your business until you get their attention and give them a reason to care.

ACTION: *Why would anyone care about what you do? How can your marketing be reworked to make them care?*

_____

_____

_____

_____

_____

_____

_____

_____

DAY THREE

Creativity is a great way to make your message "sticky" - to help customers retain it long enough to act on it. But sometimes, the message itself is so simple and powerful that it can stand alone. Case in point: a recent bank ad tries to be clever to get the idea across that they're open on Sundays. But since a lot of banks are closed on Sunday, is it possible that "Now Open Sundays" is the best way to make that point? Marketing needs to be creative and engaging when you're differentiating yourself from the competition. But when the way you do business differentiates you all by itself, let it do the heavy lifting.

ACTION: *Are you different than your competitors in some significant and really unique way? If so, shout it out as clearly as possible. If not, why not?*

_____

_____

_____

_____

_____

_____

_____

_____

DAY FOUR

Trust is a valuable — and increasingly rare — asset in business. And if you look at the companies that enjoy the highest trust from customers, they tend to be run by enthusiasts rather than numbers people. People trust Apple more than Microsoft because Steve Jobs was wildly enthusiastic about what Apple made. You probably trust a recommendation from your local bookstore more than one from an employee at a big chain. General Motors was much more trusted when it was run by "car guys" rather than "numbers guys."

ACTION: *Are you an enthusiast? Do your customers know it? How can you be sure your enthusiasm shows through in your marketing??*

_____

_____

_____

_____

_____

_____

_____

_____

DAY FIVE

Every year, right around Super Bowl time, a phenomenon occurs that is nearly non-existent the rest of the year. Companies actually promote their ads across other platforms. And it works. A lot more people see the ads — and if they're good, a lot more people buy stuff. So why doesn't this happen all year? And why don't you do it? If you create advertising that people will want to see (you do, don't you?), let them know to watch for it.

ACTION: *Make your message intensely watchable, then have CSRs ask every customer if they've seen it. Promote it on social media. Have your team give it a shout-out via e-mail. Spread the word.*

_____

_____

_____

_____

_____

_____

_____

_____

DAY ONE

Ron Howard's 1995 film may have immortalized the phrase, "Houston, we have a problem," but it did something else - it showed us a model of innovation. With their vehicle crippled in an accident, the crew of Apollo 13 has to find a solution quickly to avoid tragedy. On the ground, the NASA team is given exactly what the astronauts have on board, and told to find a solution. This "limitation" narrowed their focus and kept them on track. The same principle should be at work in your business. Innovation is the most under-utilized way to succeed, but meaningful innovation comes when the goal and constraints are clearly laid out.

ACTION: *Where is one opportunity for innovation in your business right now? What are the constraints? What's the potential? Where do you start?*

_____

_____

_____

_____

_____

_____

_____

DAY TWO

Who you compare yourself to defines who you are. Author Seth Godin once blogged about the one restaurant in the Atlanta airport that managed to delight him (One Flew South in Terminal E). How does this one eatery rise above the mediocrity of its peers? The general manager explained to Godin, "We don't compare ourselves to other airport restaurants." What if a doctor's office compared its service to a spa? Or a hospital compared its food to a restaurant's?

ACTION: *When you set the bar for your company, change yardsticks. If you want to improve customer service, who would you compare yourself to?*

_____

_____

_____

_____

_____

_____

_____

_____

_____

DAY THREE

A recent news story cited "the difficulty of developing consensus around how to solve the intractable problem of youth violence." But complex problems are rarely solved by consensus. Breakthrough ideas — the kind that are truly radical — almost never emerge from a group setting. Albert Einstein, an idea man if ever there was one, observed, "If at first the idea is not absurd, then there is no hope for it." Consensus certainly has a place, but truly game-changing ideas never survive the consensus-building process. If you're looking for ways to create dramatic change in the way you do business, keep in mind that there are always many more people who can tell you why an idea won't work than there are people who can come up with a better one.

ACTION: *What matters more in your business: getting buy-in from a lot of people, or coming up with world-class, game-changing ideas? Does your process for developing new ideas reflect this? You are developing new ideas, aren't you?*

DAY FOUR

On an episode of "Mad Men," the AMC series set in a 1960s ad agency, a copywriter finds inspiration for a campaign in the middle of the night. Drinking to his own success, he drifts off, and when he's awakened the next morning, the idea has slipped back into the ether. Every business needs ideas. And everyone knows that the best ideas often arrive in the shower, on the edge of sleep, in the car — anywhere but behind a desk. The simple step of being prepared to capture them - having pen and paper or a recorder in the places ideas usually arrive - can be the least expensive and most profound competitive advantage you'll ever find.

ACTION: *Ask yourself — and your team — where you are when you get your best ideas. Then brainstorm good ways to make sure you capture and collect those ideas — and put them into action.*

DAY FIVE

Most businesses hope to lure prospects from a competitor. In fact, it's one of only three ways you can grow (the others to get more business from the customers you have now, or to create something so new that there is no competition). But ask yourself this: what would make *you* switch? What would it take to get you to change banks, doctors, cleaners, printers or car dealers? If you really want to overcome a prospect's inertia, you'll never it do it by claiming to be as good as the provider they use now. Here's what will work. Do something your competitors don't. It's hard, but simple. Find the thing they're overlooking, or something they haven't thought of, and pour your heart (and your marketing muscle) into it.

ACTION: *Set time aside to brainstorm everything you could start doing that none of your competitors do. Make sure they're things that matter to potential customers. How many could you offer? What are the barriers? How can you overcome them? When will you start?*

_____

_____

_____

_____

_____

_____

_____

DAY ONE

When we face a difficult business challenge, our first response is usually to look around our own industry to see how other companies like ours have solved it. This poses two problems. First, your challenge is often shared by others, but truly solved by no one. Second, it limits the solution to whatever your competitors are doing. Instead, consider how other industries are solving tangentially similar problems. While HBO and Showtime began as movie channels, they discovered that the key to the future was developing original series like "The Sopranos," "The Wire," "Game of Thrones" and "Homeland."

ACTION: *Think of one persistent challenge you face. Now look at industries other than yours who have dealt with — and overcome — similar challenges. How can you apply what they've done to your business?*

DAY TWO

No matter the medium, if you can engage more of your audience's senses, your message is a lot stickier. If a radio spot invites you to smell something cooking, or a TV spot lingers on silky skin, the effectiveness of those messages goes up dramatically. It's a great creative challenge that yields real marketing results.

ACTION: *How can you engage at least one additional sense in your next marketing message?*

_____

_____

_____

_____

_____

_____

_____

_____

_____

_____

DAY THREE

Why do your customers come back for more? Is there a saturation point where they've taken advantage of all your services, or where there's nothing new for them to see or try? Think of the way animals forage. They eat all the available food in a relatively small area, then move on, pick a new area and start over. Consumers aren't much different. If we believe that a store, shop, restaurant, etc. hasn't changed since the last time we visited, we're less likely to return. The challenge for business, whether selling consumer products, business services or something else, is to constantly introduce something new to cause customers to come back. This needs to become part of your company's DNA if you're going to succeed over the long term.

ACTION: *What's your process for regularly coming up with new reasons for customers or clients to return to you?*

_____

_____

_____

_____

_____

_____

_____

DAY FOUR

Scott Ackerson, a producer for ESPN, recalls trying to fill a 7-minute hole in a Sunday edition of "Sportscenter" during the British Open. He arranged a short interview with golf legend Jack Nicklaus about the state of his sport. The following week, during the Davis Cup, the same scenario occurred, and he filled the time with a similar chat with tennis star John McEnroe. Executive VP John Walsh commented that he liked the two segments, and "Sunday Conversation" became a regular part of SportsCenter's programming. It pays to recognize the happy accidents that can turn into long-term successes. More important, it pays to remember that if you don't try new ideas, you can't harvest new successes.

ACTION: *Is there a systematic way for your team to share their "happy accidents" — things they did in the moment that turned out surprisingly well? How can you create a way for those ideas to go viral within your organization?*

_____

_____

_____

_____

_____

_____

_____

DAY FIVE

One of the ways Walt Disney continued to push the creative envelope was to encourage his people to "plus" one another's ideas. Rather then have ideas presented in isolation by whomever came up with it, Disney prompted his people to add to one another's ideas so they got even bigger. While this runs counter to the competitive nature of most businesses, it created a culture of shared creativity at Disney that made the company iconic.

ACTION: *What happens to ideas to your company? Are they cause for enthusiastic sharing and enlarging, or do they remain in isolation? (Or worst of all, are they discouraged?) Bigger ideas build business (and your brand) faster.*

_____

_____

_____

_____

_____

_____

_____

DAY ONE

Companies often talk about developing extraordinary products or delivering an extraordinary customer experience. But few actually do it - because offering something extraordinary means *doing something extra.* The baseline is doing everything as well as it can be done - then adding something truly unique on top of that. Think of Apple - they build the most reliable devices around, then add fantastic design, cool stores and innovative extras that keep competitors racing to catch up.

ACTION: *What "extra" would / could you offer to become extraordinary? Because extraordinary is profitable.*

_____

_____

_____

_____

_____

_____

_____

_____

DAY TWO

When a business hires a new marketing person or a new agency, there's almost always a "honeymoon" period when the new recruit's ideas and recommendations are greeted with enthusiasm and green lights. With the passing of time, the honeymoon ends and that enthusiastic approval recedes into the distance, taking with it the opportunity to keep the brand energized and customers engaged. What if yours was the company that worked to keep the romance alive — to continue to encourage and welcome fresh thinking from your marketing people and partners? You might be surprised at the positive effect it has on your P&L statement.

ACTION: *Ask your marketing team if they feel that new ideas are enthusiastically encouraged. How can you ensure that they are?*

_____

_____

_____

_____

_____

_____

_____

DAY THREE

Companies often look to the stars in their own industries to identify best practices or innovations they can adopt for their own growth. But adaptation — looking at the ways in which companies or industries outside your own have solved problems or created opportunities, then adapting those ideas to your own business — can yield solutions you would never find among your peers. For example, imagine a banking conference where all of the speakers are from successful companies outside banking. What insights could be gained from the ways other industries see the world?

ACTION: *Think of a problem you need to solve or an opportunity you want to create. How can you look outside your industry for inspiration?*

_____

_____

_____

_____

_____

_____

_____

_____

DAY FOUR

When ESPN was still just an idea, an HBO executive dismissed it, saying, "There's no way anyone will ever watch sports 24 hours a day." Today, the sports network, owned by Disney, accounts for 28% of the entertainment giant's stock value, and is considered a prized cash cow. The lesson for businesses? You're defined not only by the ideas you embrace, but by those you dismiss. And since rejecting new ideas is a lot easier than exploring them, most companies miss a lot of opportunities.

ACTION: *Do you encourage new ideas, even those that might initially seem far-fetched? Or is your office the place where ideas go to die?*

DAY FIVE

The average personal injury trial has a lot to do with motivation. The defense lawyers are paid for their time, but the prosecution gets a big slice of any judgment. More risk, but potentially higher returns. So who do you think works harder? Same with established companies and new ones. If you've been around for awhile, young, hungry competitors are likely to focus on taking your customers, while you focus on not losing them. Different motivations, different energy levels and different outcomes.

ACTION: *What would change if you marketed like the young upstart? What are three things you could do over the course of the next six months to amp up the energy and motivational levels in your company?*

_____

_____

_____

_____

_____

_____

_____

DAY ONE

When a small group of music lovers started Numero Group, the idea was to find great lost records and release them in small quantities on CD and vinyl. A classic "long tail" business, they're not trying to find million sellers; they can be profitable selling 10,000 copies. But one of their smart innovations is to borrow a page from the magazine industry and sell subscriptions. For an annual subscription fee, you get every release the label puts out. Numero's fans include actress / singer Zooey Deschanel and former Led Zeppelin frontman Robert Plant.

ACTION: *What unconventional delivery system could you appropriate from a completely different industry to increase sales?*

_____

_____

_____

_____

_____

_____

_____

_____

DAY TWO

It's amazing how many great innovations have their origin in anger or frustration. When the late Ermal Fraze was frustrated because no one had brought a can opener to a picnic, he invented the pull-tab to open soda cans. When he was frustrated at seeing all those pull tabs on the ground, he invented today's pop-top, where the tab stays on the can. If it annoys you, it probably annoys other people, too.

ACTION: *What annoyance could you eliminate through innovation? Now add the words "for your customers" after the word "eliminate." If you can answer that question - and act on it - you're about to make a lot of money.*

_____

_____

_____

_____

_____

_____

_____

_____

_____

DAY THREE

It's no secret that physicians are reimbursed less these days for the care they provide. Sooner or later, more doctors are going to turn into niche marketers. Imagine a pediatrician's practice that only makes house calls - and only to private pay clients. Maybe there are two doctors who stagger shifts so they cover everything from 7 AM to 8 PM. House calls are available on weekends, but at a higher rate, and it's all billed to a credit card. Certainly that's a narrow market, but they don't need volume if they price their services right. Office expense is minimal, since they make house calls, so overhead is lower. And once one doctor does this successfully, others will follow.

ACTION: *Is there a niche you can innovate your way into? How?*

_____

_____

_____

_____

_____

_____

_____

_____

DAY FOUR

Payroll cards are such a simple idea, it's astonishing they haven't become commonplace already. Employees receive a debit card that gets recharged with their net pay each pay period. What does this eliminate the need for? Checking accounts, service charges and overdraft fees, to name a few. If you're a bank, this innovation stands to cost you a lot of money.

ACTION: *Is there some innovation brewing that could make what you offer less important or even obsolete? If so, how can you shift gears toward that business model — or away from it and into something completely different?*

DAY FIVE

One of the subtle obstacles to innovation or change is "conventional wisdom." Once an idea or position is accepted as conventional, it escapes all scrutiny. Ironically, those widely-held beliefs are often hiding opportunity; it's just that no one is looking. So it pays to examine the conventional wisdom in your company or industry, and discover whether your next opportunity might be lurking there unnoticed.

ACTION: *What assumptions or principles are accepted as conventional wisdom in your industry — or even in your company? If you set that aside, what opportunities can you uncover?*

_____

_____

_____

_____

_____

_____

_____

_____

DAY ONE

To promote its vampire series, "True Blood," HBO put up signs that read, "In Case of Vampire." The signs have rows of wooden stakes attached that can be snapped off. What was really a windfall for HBO was the number of people who took pictures of the signs and posted them online via social media. So while the signs may have been a little more expensive to produce than traditional ones, the multiplier effect made them cheap by comparison.

ACTION: *How can you come up with an unconventional medium to use, or unconventional ways to use that medium, to promote what you sell — or some benefit of what you sell?*

_____

_____

_____

_____

_____

_____

_____

DAY TWO

Let's start by saying that if you don't already have a plan in place to deliver value to customers and prospects through regular e-mail, you're extremely late to the party. With that out of the way, here's a number you can use to measure your own efforts. The average open rate for e-mail campaigns still hovers around 20% (and higher for some industries - check the stats to see the norm for what you do).

ACTION: *Check your own open rates to see how you stack up — above average or below? Second, compare it to other media. Is your print ad read by 20% of subscribers? Is your radio spot heard by 20% of listeners? Is your billboard seen by 20% of drivers?*

_____

_____

_____

_____

_____

_____

_____

DAY THREE

A blogger recently used the phrase "media agnostic," and it seemed timely - and timeless. When it comes to marketing your business, you have to let go of any devotion (or aversion) to any particular medium. Whatever works is the best tool to use. It might be something on the leading edge of digital, or something that's been around for centuries. More likely, it's a combination of the two with a powerful, integrated message.

ACTION: *Ask yourself this question: if you were told today that you had to let go of the one medium you think has been least successful for you, what would it be?*

_____

_____

_____

_____

_____

_____

_____

_____

_____

DAY FOUR

The number of smartphone and tablet owners continues to grow dramatically. And as more of these users read e-mail and access the internet via their mobile devices, marketers will need to re-think their e-mail strategies and websites. How does the e-mail blast you just sent appear on a smartphone? How does that same user see your website on such a small screen? Is there an app to help you help your customers more easily?

ACTION: *What do you need to do now to stay ahead of this swiftly-moving trend — especially if you're targeting a younger, more mobile audience?*

DAY FIVE

A key element of any e-mail marketing strategy is building your list.

ACTION: *If someone visits your website, how easy is it for them to subscribe to your e-mails? Is that link one of the very first things they see, or is it buried somewhere? Do you have a sample of your e-mails on the site so they can check it out before subscribing? Those two actions alone can have a huge impact on how quickly your e-mail list grows. And don't forget traditional media. If you're using print advertising or direct mail, for example, do they encourage readers to sign up?*

_____

_____

_____

_____

_____

_____

_____

_____

_____

DAY ONE

If you're going to use Twitter (or any social medium), remember that you're not giving a speech; you're trying to start a conversation. Instead of relentless self-promotion, consider what you can tweet or post that will be a benefit to those who follow you. Can you pass along new information or helpful tips they can use to improve their lives or their businesses? Can you pose a thoughtful question, or ask for an opinion? Can you surprise or delight? Sweeten those tweets and see who you attract.

ACTION: *How can you make sure that your social media efforts are focused firmly on creating relevant conversations or curating helpful information?*

_____

_____

_____

_____

_____

_____

_____

_____

_____

DAY TWO

If you're on the fence about building an active social media presence, consider this. A quarter of Americans' time online is spent with social media and blogs. When people try to learn more about a product or company, over half use the company's social media pages to find out about them. And nearly half of those have responded to a company's offer through Twitter or Facebook. All these trends suggest that your social media presence is becoming as important as your website in providing a way for new prospects to learn about you.

ACTION: *Does your social media presence represent your brand as robustly and consistently as your website or other marketing materials? What can you start doing differently today to improve it?*

_____

_____

_____

_____

_____

_____

_____

DAY THREE

You may not think of it this way, but your website is the perfect vehicle for weeding out prospects, either intentionally or accidentally. If you're targeting a very narrow audience — very high income consumers with specific interests, or corporations above a certain size — say so on your site, and steer away those who wouldn't qualify. On the other hand, take a good look to be sure that your site isn't accidentally discouraging the very people or businesses you want to attract. Either way, your website should be generating leads for you.

ACTION: *Is your website attracting the right audience and steering the wrong one away? Is it generating leads? If not, what changes can you make to ensure that it does?*

_____

_____

_____

_____

_____

_____

_____

DAY FOUR

Especially with a company's first website, navigation is often designed around what the company wants people to know. This is often compounded by the lack of a real, organized plan for how the site should flow. The result is a site that's hard to navigate, with links that lead to dead ends or pages that you can only find through sheer luck — then never find again. So visitors leave.

ACTION: *If you were going to review one aspect of your website today, a great place to start would be with this question: does the navigation make it as easy as possible for a prospect to find what interests them most, in as few clicks as possible? If not, how does it need to change?*

_____

_____

_____

_____

_____

_____

_____

DAY FIVE

The biggest question business people ask about Twitter is how to get followers. After all, if no one's listening, there's no point in talking. There are a number of steps you can take to create a following, but here are three of the biggest. First, start tweeting. If people do find you, you want them to see some existing content that matters to them. And use hashtags that are popular for the topic you're tweeting about. Second, follow people who tweet about your topic. Some of them will follow you back, and some of their followers will tag along. Third, include the Twitter logo and link in every marketing message.

ACTION: *Who in your company is responsible for your Twitter output? How do you monitor and measure it? How strong is your system for tweeting consistently with ideas or observations that are relevant to your audience?*

_____

_____

_____

_____

_____

_____

_____

DAY ONE

Whenever companies resist the idea of starting a blog or participating in Facebook or Twitter, it's often for one of two reasons. The first: they don't want to open the door to negative comments from the outside. But if something about your business prompts a negative response, those comments are happening anyway. When you have a social media presence, they happen in a place where you can see them and respond. You might even gain insights into your company that help you get better. But avoiding social media to avoid criticism is just sticking your head in the sand.

ACTION: *Why might you be avoiding social media? Does this suggest changes you need to make to your business? Can social media help you communicate those changes more effectively?*

_____

_____

_____

_____

_____

_____

_____

DAY TWO

Another reason companies resist social media is that they can't imagine how they'll be able to come up with new content. That's because they haven't answered the bigger question: *why*? Why give yourself this new forum? What do you want to accomplish? Do you want to educate consumers? Do you want a sounding board for your ideas? Do you want to start a conversation about what you do? If you begin with a purpose, a goal you want to accomplish, the content ideas will come.

ACTION: *What can you accomplish through social media that you can't do any other way for the same investment (in time or money)? How will this direct your social efforts?*

_____

_____

_____

_____

_____

_____

_____

_____

DAY THREE

The more a visitor can do from your website, the more likely it is that your website is selling for you. Can a visitor ask a question? Sign up for a newsletter? Follow a blog? Download a whitepaper? Follow you on social media? Take a survey? Buy something? The more ways you can engage that visitor, the more likely they are to become a customer, or to do more with you than they already do.

ACTION: *Take a look at your website and list all the ways it engages your visitors? What's missing? Add one new means of engagement to your site this quarter — and schedule one more for each of the next two quarters.*

DAY FOUR

Recent research shows that prospects are now about 60% through the decision-making process before they ever talk to a salesperson. How do they get that far? Online, of course. What that means is that your website is either making or breaking your chances of winning a customer long before your salespeople get a shot. And when you consider that a lot of that process is happening on mobile devices like smartphones and (increasingly) tablets, it lends real urgency to the task of critiquing your site and making it sell harder.

ACTION: *How good a salesperson is your website? What can you change to make it better?*

_____

_____

_____

_____

_____

_____

_____

DAY FIVE

Fear of falling behind is a terrible thing. It makes a lot of companies feel like they have to jump on a marketing idea just because it's the cool thing or everyone seems to be doing it. But what if creating a 6-second vine doesn't do anything for your business at all? Digital media has this in common with traditional media: you have to be choosy. Cool is fine if it builds your brand or brings in business, but most of the time, it just cuts into cash flow.

ACTION: *Are you spending time and money on media that's a cool new trend but isn't really doing anything for your business? If so, cut it out — and put your resources into something more beneficial.*

DAY ONE

A recent visit to a restaurant's revamped website turned up a lot of stuff. But not the restaurant's hours. Now think about why people visit a restaurant's website. It's a pretty safe bet that finding the restaurant's hours is one of the top reasons to visit, along with a menu and directions. Yet several people worked on or approved this site, and no one thought that hours might be important. Unfortunately, it's a common malady. Companies tend to put the information on their websites that they want people to know, rather than what the potential customer needs to know.

ACTION: *Who is your website for? Does your content match what your potential customers want to know? Could you ask customers what they want to see?*

_____

_____

_____

_____

_____

_____

_____

_____

DAY TWO

A trend in website design is to cram everything you can onto every page.
It's a bad trend. Even if a lot of companies are doing it (mostly to attract
search engines), it seldom makes sense. A site can quickly become cluttered
and push visitors away. Organize your site the way a visitor would. What
do they most want to know about? Have the information that matters in
a very obvious place. Make it easy for visitors to dig deeper if they choose.
Minimize the number of clicks it takes to reach important content. And
write in a way that appeals to both the audience and the search engines.

ACTION: *Have several people who have never seen your website sit down and
go through it, making notes about their reactions and experience. Then have your
own people do the same. Compare notes — but give more weight to the outsiders.*

_____

_____

_____

_____

_____

_____

_____

_____

DAY THREE

If social media is an important component of your marketing effort, don't just use it to pitch your business. Instead, ask yourself what you can give. What valuable information, insights or ideas can you pass along to your readers, connections, fans or followers? What would change if they saw your social media sites as places to get what they need? If you put their value first, there's a good chance you'll have a more engaged audience — and an easier time selling when it's time to sell.

ACTION: *What do your prospects want or need to know? How can you help them with information or resources — even links to other websites.*

_____

_____

_____

_____

_____

_____

_____

_____

DAY FOUR

One often-overlooked benefit of online and social media is how easy it makes it to keep up with your competitors. Now it's a simple matter to subscribe to your rivals' e-mails or blog posts, follow them on Facebook or LinkedIn — even see what their own customers are saying about them. It's just one more reason — as if another was needed — to make social media a vital element in your overall marketing program.

ACTION: *Schedule time every week for monitoring your competitor's social media. Use what you see for your own internal discussions about how you can compete more effectively.*

_____

_____

_____

_____

_____

_____

_____

_____

DAY FIVE

If you're using social media to engage customers, influencers and prospects, are you asking them to help? You'd be surprised how much more quickly your message will spread if you encourage that behavior.

ACTION: *Request retweets and offer a good reason to do so. Ask Facebook fans to invite friends to an event or share a special offer. Include an ask or invitation, and put more social into your media.*

_____

_____

_____

_____

_____

_____

_____

_____

_____

_____

DAY ONE

Around 1980, Kodak did research that showed that the preference for film over digital photography would last through the 1980s. And it did. But instead of using that decade to shift gears, Kodak's management used the study to cling to film and continued to regard digital photography as the enemy — *in spite of the fact that its own engineers developed technology that is crucial to digital cameras today.* The result? Digital photos improved dramatically, prices plunged and everyone got used to looking at photos onscreen — all of which left Kodak in the lurch.

ACTION: *Take a different look at your own "enemies." How can you change your stance or direction and embrace the future before it makes you irrelevant?*

_____

_____

_____

_____

_____

_____

_____

_____

DAY TWO

Sure, Walgreen's Health & Wellness division is smart. The in-store clinics, staffed by a nurse practitioner, can treat patients faster and cheaper for everyday maladies. And while the clinics are self-supporting profit centers (they pass break-even in 2 to 3 years), the big bonus is that nearly a third of patients become new customers for Walgreen's pharmacies. But the big move now is placing Walgreen's clinics onsite in large employers, often with primary care physicians on staff. Clearly, the retail chain is taking a broader view of what it does.

ACTION: *Spend some time defining the current limits and boundaries in your business. Then explore ways you can profitably exceed those limits or break those boundaries.*

DAY THREE

Reed Hastings was always frustrated when his local video store was out of the movie he wanted. But when he got tagged with a $40 late fee for a movie he'd misplaced, it got him thinking. What if everyone shared his frustration with video stores? On his way to the gym, it hit him. Gyms charge a flat monthly fee. Why not video stores? Why not by mail, so the movie you want is always in stock? And Netflix was born.

ACTION: *Look at your own business. What about it is universally frustrating for customers? You don't have to start a new company; just reinvent the way yours serves customers.*

_____

_____

_____

_____

_____

_____

_____

_____

DAY FOUR

When you can order from thousands of choices on Netflix or browse a ton of titles on Amazon or iTunes, how could Redbox — the DVD kiosks you see at McDonald's and supermarkets — stand a chance? They saw a niche and filled it. They were in more locations (in other words, more convenient) than Blockbuster ever was. You got your DVD faster (more convenient, again) than with Netflix (before Netflix created its online presence, at least). And here's the clincher. Since most people rent movies between 4 and 9 PM, the kiosks are located at the other places people frequent during that time slot: grocery stores and restaurants. Convenience, again. Streaming video will someday retire Redbox, but not until it makes a boatload of money by being convenient.

ACTION: *Can you introduce convenience as a competitive advantage? How?*

_____

_____

_____

_____

_____

_____

_____

DAY FIVE

Most companies of any size make a lot of small contributions to various charities during a given year. But what if every company picked a single nonprofit whose cause meshed well with their business, then created a program to involve customers and generate support for that charity. There are plenty of examples. Kellogg set up a page on its website where consumers who donate $5 or more to Feeding America can receive $5 in coupons for Kellogg cereals. With no shortage of local charities needing a hand, how can you find one that makes sense for your brand, then redirect your charitable giving so that you help the nonprofit financially, raise awareness for its mission and give your own business a boost?

ACTION: *Ask your team their thoughts and come up with three local charities that you could help financially. Now list different reasons why each charity would be the best fit for your company to invest in...and start giving.*

_____

_____

_____

_____

_____

_____

_____

DAY ONE

Many marketing budgets are created backwards. Some "standard" is applied, such as the industry average for companies your size, or a fixed percentage of income - then marketing expenses are shoe-horned into that number.

ACTION: *What if you did the opposite? What if you began by defining your goals (sales, customers, retention, etc.), then built a strategic plan designed to offer the best chance of meeting or beating those goals – THEN attached dollar amounts to that plan to arrive at a budget? What would that process look like? What if that process actually resulted in a smaller, but more focused budget?*

_____

_____

_____

_____

_____

_____

_____

_____

_____

DAY TWO

Have you (or more likely, your kids) ever heard an ice cream truck, scrambled for some cash and dashed out the door, only to find the truck receding in the distance? Makes you wonder why some enterprising ice cream truck driver doesn't figure out which neighborhoods offer the best potential (lots of houses close together, plenty of signs of kids), then make up a schedule, print it up and slip it into paper boxes. Parents and kids then know when to expect a frosty treat to roll by, and the driver makes much more money per mile.

ACTION: *So back to you – are you making it easy for people to do business with you? Could you make it easier and make more money? How?*

_____

_____

_____

_____

_____

_____

_____

_____

DAY THREE

Sometimes you have to recognize when your own rule works against you. A recent blog post observed that most concerts begin with the obligatory ban on cameras and recording devices. Not a Wiggles concert. The silly, snug-shirted kids' combo started by encouraging the audience to take all the pictures and video they want - and to share them with friends. This, of course, turned thousands of adoring fans into mini-marketers.

ACTION: *Is there some sacred cow or widely accepted convention in your industry that you could turn upside down for fun and profit? (Hint: the answer is "yes!") Your job is simply to find one and exploit it.*

_____

_____

_____

_____

_____

_____

_____

_____

_____

DAY FOUR

Here's Proctor & Gamble's purpose: "We will provide branded products of superior quality and value that improve the lives of the world's consumers, now and for generations to come." Now get this part: "As a result, consumers will reward us with leadership sales, profit and value creations, allowing our people, our shareholders and the communities in which we live and work to prosper." In other words, the 171-year old company ties its success directly to making people's lives better.

ACTION: *If delivering value drives success, it pays to see if your company's priorities are in the right order. What does your company do to add value to the lives of your customers? How can you make this your first focus?*

_____

_____

_____

_____

_____

_____

_____

DAY FIVE

In the Mel Gibson film, *We Were Soldiers*, there's a re-telling of a battle in Vietnam where American troops were at a clear disadvantage. They found themselves in a valley, completely surrounded, and vastly outnumbered by an enemy who held the high ground around them and had an uninterrupted supply line. All their opponents lacked was focus. American Lt. Col. Hal Moore realized that his optimistic enemy had an "attack anywhere" offensive approach, but no strategy whatsoever for defense. By focusing his men in a concentrated assault on the enemy's hilltop command center, the Americans defeated a much larger enemy.

ACTION: *Where should your focus be today: on everything or on one thing? If the latter, what's that one thing? How will that focus change what you're doing?*

_____

_____

_____

_____

_____

_____

_____

_____

DAY ONE

We often assume that when it comes to serving customers, the more choices we offer, the better. But studies show that having too many options can cause consumers to choose nothing at all. For example, a study of 401k plans found that as the number of investment choices in a plan rise, participation falls.

ACTION: *If you're offering your customers a choice of products or services, focus on a smaller array of options, but make each option more appealing.*

_____

_____

_____

_____

_____

_____

_____

_____

_____

DAY TWO

"He who does not gather with me, scatters." (Matt. 12:30) One of the great dangers of a sluggish economy is that it tempts us to believe we can operate in neutral for a time — that we can coast with no real negative consequence. If you were operating in a vacuum, that might be true. But as you mark time, the competition, consumer needs and demands and a hundred other variables all remain in motion. Like it or not, your business is either moving forward or slipping backward.

ACTION *If neutral isn't an option, how can you be sure your company stays in drive? How does this change how you market?*

_____

_____

_____

_____

_____

_____

_____

_____

DAY THREE

The inspired choice Apple made when setting up the Genius Bar in its retail stores is that it works on so many levels. First, consider employees. Which would you rather be called: technical support, customer service or a genius? And let's face it, a bar just sounds better than a department, counter or help desk. Now think like a customer. If you have a problem or a question, who do you want to talk with, tech support or a genius? And which one sets a better expectation?

ACTION: *What you call something really matters. How can you use this to reshape internal and external perceptions of your brand?*

_____

_____

_____

_____

_____

_____

_____

_____

DAY FOUR

If you're developing a name for a new business or a new product, here are two reasons to make up a word from scratch. First, assuming the made-up word has the right "feel," you get to create the meaning. Starbucks is a great example; completely meaningless, but now infused with the meaning they wanted it to have. Likewise Viagra. Second, a word created from scratch has a certain search engine magic. If it didn't exist before you made it up, then guess who pops up first when you do an online search? You guessed it. Remember - a name you make up won't dazzle you or anyone at first. Nike didn't. Apple didn't. Yours won't. It's what you make of it that matters.

ACTION: *If you're naming a company or product, what qualities does it need to embody? What are all the words that describe that quality? How can you modify or mix portions of those words to create something new?*

_____

_____

_____

_____

_____

_____

_____

DAY FIVE

In the family film, *We Bought a Zoo*, Matt Damon's character shares a
tip with his teenage son. If you're nervous about doing something, force
yourself to put all your fear aside and plunge ahead for twenty seconds, with
no regard for how embarrassing it may turn out. That twenty seconds is
often just enough time to get you safely to the other side of awkward, and
free you to do what you wanted to do. If you're not a natural networker,
and the thought of approaching a total stranger makes you cringe, try it.
Give it everything you have for twenty seconds. Chances are, that's enough
time for the person you approach to smile and shake hands, and you're over
the hump.

ACTION: *Can you endure twenty awkward seconds? What are you holding back
from? Can you give it your all for a third of a minute?*

_____

_____

_____

_____

_____

_____

_____

DAY ONE

Look at a new pencil — about 7" of lead and a quarter-inch eraser. Now maybe that's all that works structurally. But what expectation does it set? That we make very few mistakes, and then remove all traces of them. But for a learning organization, mistakes are how we course-correct. The CEO of one Fortune 500 company famously said that if he had senior people who hadn't made a single big blunder over the years, they should be fired — because they clearly weren't taking any chances of consequence.

ACTION: *Are you and those around you expected to take chances...even if some of them may fail spectacularly? Does everyone know this?*

_____

_____

_____

_____

_____

_____

_____

_____

DAY TWO

Companies often look to a tagline to develop their brand. The problem? Most taglines — which should really be viewed as brand promises — slip away into empty sloganeering. Think about the tagline that launched Federal Express: "When it absolutely, positively has to be there overnight." This is the trick — to position yourself as, in this case, the dependability guys without actually using the overused word itself.

ACTION: *What does your tagline say about you? Is it a promise? Does it promise something customers value highly? Can your brand keep it?*

DAY THREE

Sometimes the words we use carry more weight than we'd like. When you "open" an account at a bank or credit union, it's the start of something. The expectation is that you'll use your account to make purchases or save for future dreams. But when a loan is "closed," it feels like the end of something. All that lies ahead are years of payments. And a lot of that is the financial institution's fault. That loan — for a home or a business — could be the start of something, too. Happy memories. Company growth. And other ways the bank or credit union could be part of your life. But too often, it's just a closing.

ACTION: *When do you close the chapter on customers when you really want to turn the page? How can you change it?*

_____

_____

_____

_____

_____

_____

_____

DAY FOUR

On a recent Saturday at a skate park, one thing was abundantly clear. Kids trying to execute something new on a skateboard or bike stumble or fall much more often than they succeed. And it almost always hurts. Does that stop them? Absolutely not. They turn right around and take another run at it. And the other kids cheer even the most epic failures with encouragement and praise for the attempt. So why is it that the grown-ups in business can't behave that way? Maybe we forget what kids know: the path to success is paved with repeated failures. They don't fear failure yet; that's something we teach them later.

ACTION: *How can you unlearn that most unproductive of lessons and encourage the failures that lead to big successes — for yourself and your team?*

_____

_____

_____

_____

_____

_____

_____

DAY FIVE

We often want to know why the prospects who didn't buy from us made that decision? But the flaw in that question lies in its answer. If they say it was price, we think we need to lower our prices. But the truth is, we don't know what *would* have made them buy from us — unless we ask. Maybe it wasn't a lower price, but better features for the money or more convenience — in other words, a better *value*, as the prospect sees value.

ACTION: *Asking this one question — what would have made you a customer — can turn the loss of a sale into a really valuable lesson. Are you asking? Can you start? How?*

_____

_____

_____

_____

_____

_____

_____

_____

_____

DAY ONE

Moms control 85% of all household spending. But nearly three quarters of them believe marketers don't understand them — and 60% think marketers simply ignore their needs. And increasingly, the way to reach those moms is online. That's especially true of younger mothers, who spend more time online than with radio, magazines and newspapers *combined*. A majority of moms of all ages follow blogs, use social networks, shop and pay bills online, and stay in touch with family and friends that way.

ACTION: *If moms make up some or all of your target market, how does your marketing need to change to let them know you get it? What are you missing?*

_____

_____

_____

_____

_____

_____

_____

_____

DAY TWO

Too often, businesses behave as though there's one big, homogeneous market. So a great first step in making your marketing more effective (and this is true whether you sell to other businesses or consumers) is to divide your target audience into segments with similar needs and interests. For example, if you're selling bank services, a mature widow, a 40-something entrepreneur and a recent college graduate need very different things and have divergent interests and behaviors. Understanding this helps you target each more precisely and market more cost-effectively.

ACTION: *Take a close look at your existing customer. How many specific market segments can you identify — groups who share common characteristics you can use to reach them more accurately and communicate more persuasively?*

_____

_____

_____

_____

_____

_____

_____

_____

DAY THREE

While television in particular has relentlessly pursued the 18 - 34 age group, here's something to think about. The baby boomers, all of whom are now age 50 and above, generate over 40% of all disposable income in the U.S., buy half of all new cars and 60% of packaged goods — and are online 3.5 times longer each day than the national average. But most marketing — especially online marketing — skews toward youthful images and pushes this older, wealthier segment away.

ACTION: *If you'd like a share of the boomer market, think about the words and images you use — and develop those online marketing muscles.*

_____

_____

_____

_____

_____

_____

_____

_____

_____

DAY FOUR

It's a sad statistic that nearly half of all marriages end in divorce. But other than divorce lawyers, rarely does anyone consider the impact of this disappointing trend on business. It suggests that more checking accounts get opened, more appliances get sold - a lot of duplicate purchases and transactions are made as couples set up separate households. And understanding the different needs of a single mom vs. a single dad can open valuable insights into meeting those needs.

ACTION: *Is your business one that could help meet the needs of newly-single consumers, and do well by doing good? What do you need to do to start?*

_____

_____

_____

_____

_____

_____

_____

_____

_____

DAY FIVE

Would it surprise you to learn that 90% of women prefer brands they hear about from other moms? That's about twice the general consumer rate. Is there a bank anywhere in the country making a conscious effort to build word-of-mouth among moms? A law firm? A dentist?

ACTION: *How could this impact your business? What do you need to do now?*

_____

_____

_____

_____

_____

_____

_____

_____

_____

_____

DAY ONE

If you want women to respond to marketing messages, consider some basic biology. Women's brains have quadruple the connections between right and left hemispheres when compared to their male counterparts. This means intuition and emotion play a much larger role in decision making. They don't ignore logic and reason, but they more fully blend the rational and the emotional in their evaluation of the choices available to them. A company that makes women feel valued AND offers them value will win them as customers every time.

ACTION: *If women are your target audience, does your marketing reflect this significant difference in their decision-making process? If not, what changes do you need to make?*

_____

_____

_____

_____

_____

_____

_____

DAY TWO

Most companies have a certain kind of customer they want to attract: frequent buyers or those who tend to make big ticket purchases. These customers are often more sophisticated when it comes to your business. Yet most of the time, marketing material is targeted to those with only the most basic grasp of what you do.

ACTION: *If those "A" clients represent significantly higher profits, wouldn't it make sense to target your primary marketing content (brochures, website, e-mail campaigns, direct mail, etc.) specifically to these higher-value prospects? What would that look like in your business?*

_____

_____

_____

_____

_____

_____

_____

_____

DAY THREE

Over the years, bankers have had a relatively poor track record of marketing in ways that connect with women. This is truly surprising in light of the fact that women control or have primary influence over 85% of the financial transactions made in this country. Imagine this. If the bank's CEO is male, what if he wore a pregnancy suit for a week — to work, at home, at board meetings? What if you shared his experience on the website and social media? What kind of response might you get in the media and among consumers? It's just a thought.

ACTION: *Do your customers feel as though you understand them? How do you know? What's one way you can demonstrate your empathy for your target audience?*

_____

_____

_____

_____

_____

_____

_____

_____

DAY FOUR

The multi-generational household is making a comeback. Over 18% of Americans now live in a home with at least two adult generations, or a grandparent plus one or more other generations — and that percentage continues to rise. Nearly half of these households include three generations living together. While such households declined steeply from 1940 to 1980, they've been on the rise ever since.

ACTION: *If you market to consumers, these statistics beg the question: how does this affect everything from your target audience to the media you choose and the message you deliver? Is there an opportunity for your company in these numbers?*

_____

_____

_____

_____

_____

_____

_____

_____

DAY FIVE

Toys come and go as tastes change, but Legos seem perennially popular. One reason is marketing. Here's an example. In summer, the Lego website includes a Father's Day promotion that promotes the joys of bonding with your child while you build together with the colorful plastic bricks. It includes kits to build with younger or older kids - even kits Dad can build on his own. The lesson? Sometimes the long way around can lead to a quicker sale. Which is more effective: the nearly omnipresent pleading of a young Lego addict, or a tug at the heartstrings of a busy dad?

ACTION: *How can you target your audience via the people and things that matter most to them? What's the first step?*

_____

_____

_____

_____

_____

_____

_____

_____

DAY ONE

Can you expand your business by shrinking your pool of prospects? You bet. If you have a particular type of customer who is more profitable, why not position your company as one who caters exclusively to that type of customer? Fifty years ago, a laundry service had grown beyond its ability to keep up. The owner decided to scale back, so she positioned the company as a laundry service for bachelors only. Instead of shrinking, her business exploded - because she had made it exclusive to a class of high-volume customers.

ACTION: *If you had to focus on just one target audience, who would you choose? What would happen if you did?*

_____

_____

_____

_____

_____

_____

_____

DAY TWO

If you're in nearly any consumer business — health care, retail, financial — your target audience is predominantly female. And generally speaking, women respond more to value than price, especially during an economic slowdown. Women understand that paying a little more for something that will last a lot longer is a smarter purchase, especially when they factor in the time it would take to buy a replacement for the cheaper choice. If you're targeting women, especially in today's economy, you should be talking about value.

ACTION: *Do your products or services offer true value – especially value that your competitors don't offer? Do your female prospects see the value and appreciate it?*

_____

_____

_____

_____

_____

_____

_____

_____

DAY THREE

When you think of search engines, you undoubtedly think of Google, and maybe even YouTube, which surpasses even Yahoo! But what about Twitter? The social medium's search functions can help you target your message to influential consumers in your target market. For example, you can use Twitter's advanced search function to identify people within a set radius of your business who have tweeted about topics related to what you sell in the last week or month, then follow those folks with a goal of entering into an online conversation with them.

ACTION: *As social media evolve, new features continue to provide innovative ways for marketers to engage with their audiences. How many of these are you utilizing today? How do you stay abreast of what's available?*

_____

_____

_____

_____

_____

_____

_____

DAY FOUR

Every market has bloggers devoted to a particular group or subject - mom bloggers, tech bloggers, sports bloggers, culture bloggers and many, many more. Your task is two-fold: identify those bloggers who are read by your best prospects, then find ways to engage with them without overtly selling to them. SeaWorld in San Antonio invited prominent Texas mom bloggers to an exclusive, all-night, behind the scenes tour and "sleepover" with fellow bloggers. That group became friends and continues to get together. The payoff for SeaWorld (for an investment of free passes and some refreshments)? More than 3,000 positive posts about them from the bloggers most widely read by Texas moms.

ACTION: *Who's blogging about what you do? How can you interact with them in a way that benefits you both? (A word of caution: it's good to offer a blogger information or an inside look, but trying to shape their blog post about the experience is likely to backfire.)*

_____

_____

_____

_____

_____

_____

DAY FIVE

It's possible to target your audience and still use too broad a brush. For example, maybe you believe your target audience is made up of moms. Simple enough. But which moms? Homemakers or moms who work outside the home? Busy moms who put convenience at the top of their list, or moms who value qualities like organic or fair market? New moms or moms with teenagers? Urban moms or rural moms? Single moms or married moms? You get the picture. The more you can "narrowcast" your message to the people who are your true sweet spot, the bigger your marketing ROI will be.

ACTION: *How narrowly can you define your target audience? Can you break it into smaller, more specific segments? How would you market differently to each of these? Which are most profitable?*

_____

_____

_____

_____

_____

_____

_____

DAY ONE

Want to make every marketing tactic you employ more effective instantly? Here's how. Focus relentlessly on who your target audience is, what matters to them — and most of all, *what you want them to do.* Then let that focus guide every decision regarding media, creative, products and so on. Be ruthless. It will pay off.

ACTION: *What do you want your audience to do first? Do your media choices make sense for the desired action? For example, if you want someone to go to your website, media that allow them to do so immediately — e-mail, digital PPC ads — may make the most sense.*

DAY TWO

Ford's ongoing TV campaign for its truck line, voiced to perfection by actor Denis Leary, has always seemed perfectly in tune with its target audience. One spot in particular hits a high note with this intro: "If you have the kind of job where you shower *after* work…" That audience instantly recognizes itself.

ACTION: *When your prospects are exposed to your marketing, do they see right away that you "get" them? Can they instantly relate to what you're saying? If not, go back to work on your copy and capture moments that will really resonate with the audience you want.*

_____

_____

_____

_____

_____

_____

_____

_____

_____

DAY THREE

If you think only men read *Sports Illustrated*'s Swimsuit Issue, you may be surprised to learn that 18 million women read this annual publication as well. Target gets that. So when one of the models is sporting a Target bikini, the retailer often has an exclusive advertising supplement in the issue with related content, including how to buy the swimsuits you see. There's a great lesson here. It pays to set your assumptions aside and see how people are actually behaving. Then you can find less conventional — but more effective – ways to target your audience.

ACTION: *Look for opportunities to reach your audience in places other marketers haven't thought of — especially when you can be the first and obtain some measure of exclusivity. Can you find one this month?*

_____

_____

_____

_____

_____

_____

_____

_____

DAY FOUR

A salon owner did some research and found, to her surprise, that girls between ages ten and sixteen purchase the most cosmetics among all ages of women. So she gathered several groups of girls in that age group, and asked them what they liked — not just hairstyles and makeup, but music and decor as well. She then created a salon specifically for this group.

ACTION: *How sure are you that you're targeting the audience that is potentially the most profitable for you? And how do you know what they want? Those facts could unlock smart new strategic decisions.*

DAY FIVE

At a networking event, someone raised a crucial question — one you should ask yourself every day. What kind of customer are you looking for?

ACTION: *For a B2B enterprise, what does your ideal prospect look like? How much in annual sales? How many employees? How many locations? Looking for consumers? Which gender? What age? How affluent? How educated? Kids or no kids? Pets or no? Write this down. The more specific you can be, the less time, energy and money you'll waste pulling in fish you're not looking for.*

_____

_____

_____

_____

_____

_____

_____

_____

_____

_____

DAY ONE

How quickly can you name your ten biggest clients or customers? Now, just as quickly, what percentage of your total profits do they represent? If yours is like many companies, a relatively small percentage of your customer base drives the majority of your profits. More questions, then. Do these ten KNOW they're your best customers? Do they use you exclusively or is some of their business going elsewhere? Do they take advantage of everything you can do for them? Finally, do you treat them like they're your top ten? Or do you spend so much time developing new business that you leave your best clients for someone else to come along and romance?

ACTION: *Develop a component of your marketing plan designed specifically to retain your best and most profitable clients.*

_____

_____

_____

_____

_____

_____

_____

_____

DAY TWO

It runs contrary to conventional wisdom, doesn't it? Southwest Airlines is known for affordable fares. So you'd think they'd skimp on service. But they're one of the few corporations to understand that service is a function of human interaction. And Southwest's people interact with their customers with humor and genuine friendliness, even when flights are delayed or issues arise. No frills. No added expense to Southwest. Yet they remain in the black as competitors bleed red ink - and they continue to earn the highest satisfaction scores in the industry. Great service is free - and priceless.

ACTION: *Have you considered the kind of service you provide as the key to a more profitable brand? Do you know for certain how you're serving customers? Is it purposeful and sustainable? How can you make it so?*

DAY THREE

Now that cash registers do all the math, no one has to count change back to a customer anymore. Unfortunately, this has introduced an irritating, omnipresent annoyance. When you get change back today, it's bills first, then coins on top. What happens? Half the coins try to slide off the bills before you can grab them - a problem that could be easily eliminated by going old school, placing coins in the customer's palm first, followed by the bills. As annoying as the new way is, it points to a larger question.

ACTION: *Is there some little thing about the way you or your people serve customers that's a small but continual annoyance? You might want to ask around.*

_____

_____

_____

_____

_____

_____

_____

DAY FOUR

When was the last time you gave customers a nice surprise? Not a big surprise, or an expensive surprise. Just a pleasant one. There are an infinite number of ways to do this, and not one of those choices will be unappreciated by your customers. Say there's a new restaurant in town. Invite them to give you coupons for a free dessert with any entree, then distribute those to your clients. Better yet, make them branded coupons that say: "Dessert's on us." The restaurant gets traffic and awareness, your customers get free sweets and you get a little more loyalty. From a card or a phone call to a special discount day, there are literally thousands of ways to surprise customers.

ACTION: *Set aside one hour with just two or three key customer service or sales people. Spend that time doing nothing but brainstorming small ways you could surprise your customers or clients. See how many you can think of. Then identify the top four, assign a quarter to each, and implement them.*

_____

_____

_____

_____

_____

_____

DAY FIVE

From the outset, Southwest Airlines focused on major decisions — one kind of plane, one class of seat — that kept its costs lower. But low fares can be a trap. If passengers expect a lackluster experience as a result of lower fares, some will choose to pay more and get better treatment. So Southwest had a potent second ingredient: people committed to making the flying experience more pleasant - even fun. By staking out lower costs / lower fares as its core value, then creating a service culture to overcome the expectation of a service trade-off, Southwest built a brand that could win customer loyalty and survive the market turbulence that has buffeted larger and more established airlines into bankruptcy.

ACTION: *What competitive disadvantage can you compensate for with exemplary service? How can you market this so prospects recognize and desire it?*

_____

_____

_____

_____

_____

_____

_____

DAY ONE

Ask some of your best customers — the kind you'd like to have more of — to name one thing they'd change about the way you do things if they could. The answer may surprise you — and give you something you can do to retain good customers and attract more. And if it doesn't surprise you, shame on you for knowing about it and not working on it.

ACTION: *Before you begin asking customers the question noted above, ask your team what **they** think customers will say. Then ask customers. Then have a plan for using what you learn to improve your service and increase retention.*

_____

_____

_____

_____

_____

_____

_____

_____

_____

DAY TWO

If you want to be known for service, you have to answer a couple questions. First, what do customers *expect*? As fast as things change today, expectations change just as quickly, and your business has to meet those changing expectations. Second question: what would *surprise* your customers? Think of two or three ways you could surprise customers with your service delivery - then pick one and make it part of your system today. Add another in three months. It's the most reliable way to get an advantage over your competitors.

ACTION: *What is your company going to do to pleasantly surprise your customers? Once you think of something they will love, don't hesitate to do what it takes to make it happen.*

DAY THREE

A recent survey showed that boomer women are buying clothes online in rapidly increasing numbers — but *not* out of convenience. Nearly 85% cite terrible service at brick and mortar retail stores. Another big complaint — a lack of clothes they liked. Here's the takeaway: these are the customers with the most money to spend, half of whom say they buy clothes when the mood strikes, rather than waiting for sales. Retailers should be falling all over themselves to serve them. Instead, they're turning them into online shoppers, almost against their will.

ACTION: *How are you caring for your best customers? Is your service pulling them in or pushing them out? What needs to be fixed?*

DAY FOUR

One of the least expensive, most effective strategies to improve customer perceptions is easy and free: smile. If you have people in customer contact positions, step back sometime and watch how many (or how few) of them smile every time a guest walks in the door. Because smiles are increasingly rare, offering one to every client or customer is an easy way to build brand loyalty and enhance customer perceptions of your business. It works on the phone, too - customers can tell when the person on the other end of the line is smiling. Best of all, people who smile find themselves enjoying their work more - sort of a self-fulfilling prophecy.

ACTION: *Try getting all your people to smile today, and watch what happens. Maybe start with a smile of your own.*

_____

_____

_____

_____

_____

_____

_____

_____

DAY FIVE

While much has changed over the decades since Walt Disney passed on, at least one thing that was true in his day remains so today - people buy experiences. When people go to the doctor, they remember more than the diagnosis - they recall how long they had to wait, how they were treated, how they were asked for payment, how much comfort or empathy they received, whether anyone smiled at them and more.

ACTION: *Whatever you sell, keep in mind that people buy the experience. How does the experience you provide stack up? Where can you do better? Don't forget to read online reviews of your company for clues.*

_____

_____

_____

_____

_____

_____

_____

_____

DAY ONE

Think about all of the time in the past week that you've interacted with an employee of another company — the grocery store checker, a server at a restaurant, tech support and so on. How many of them seemed happy and enthusiastic? When they didn't, how did it affect your experience — and your perception of the company? Now turn that around. When people call or visit your company, how often do the people they interact with seem happy and enthusiastic? When they don't, how does it affect the customer's experience — and their perception of your company?

ACTION: *Are your people excited? Are you? It shows. How can you get them excited — and keep them that way? And remember, the back office people who serve internal customers need to be excited, too. They can set the mood for the whole operation.*

_____

_____

_____

_____

_____

_____

_____

DAY TWO

No one likes to see a customer leave. So why is it that very few companies — and virtually no small businesses — pay attention to the warning signs? Go back and take a look. What happens just before customers head for the exit? Does purchase or account activity slow? Do they unsubscribe from your e-mail list? What else?

ACTION: *If you can identify those tell-tale signs, and put a system in place to step in and contact the customer when one of the triggers is activated, you'll keep more customers — and gain a better understanding of why they ever leave.*

_____

_____

_____

_____

_____

_____

_____

_____

DAY THREE

A recent inquiry about transferring cable internet and phone service from one business location to another earned a response that was little more than a rundown of all the limitations the company placed on such a transaction, and what they couldn't do. Nothing about how excited they were to help. No offer of options. Just a flat, "these are the rules; take it or leave it" message. When the reply came that the business would shift its service back to a phone carrier, the cable rep's response? "Okay." How do you suppose their sales department, which has volume goals, would feel about that? If your people don't understand the tight connection between service and customer retention, you need to make that happen, or old clients will walk out the door as fast as new ones arrive. And that's exhausting.

ACTION: *Do you actively and regularly monitor the way your people interact with customers, especially when there's a problem? If not, how can you possibly know whether you're offering good service — and how can you improve?*

_____

_____

_____

_____

_____

_____

DAY FOUR

How does Chick-Fil-A get away with spending about a third of what McDonald's does on advertising (as a percentage of sales)? Because Chick-Fil-A focuses relentlessly on every aspect of customer service. And when people are served surprisingly well, as they often are at Chick-Fil-A, the chain can afford to spend less on advertising, because word-of-mouth is doing more of the heavy lifting. (Incidentally, there was a time when McDonald's focused relentlessly on every aspect of customer service.)

ACTION: *Do you hire with service in mind? How do you measure service? How can you reward consistent, exceptional service?*

_____

_____

_____

_____

_____

_____

_____

_____

_____

DAY FIVE

The service you provide is the key to keeping your current clients or customers happy and loyal. So here's a question to run past all your front line and service staff. What are the red flags that warn of flagging service? Just as important, what steps should be taken when those red flags are flying? And are your people free to let you know about them? As with many diseases, early detection is critical to a cure.

ACTION: *Work with staff to identify as many red flags as you can. How can you put an action plan in place for dealing with them?*

_____

_____

_____

_____

_____

_____

_____

_____

_____

DAY ONE

Press Ganey, probably the leading driver of healthcare performance improvement, analyzed patient satisfaction data to find out what matters most to patients. Getting better tops the list, right? Nope. In fact, of the top 15 criteria named by patients, *not one involved actual physical outcomes.* Every one of the 15 related to the quality of interactions between patients and staff, or to how employees seemed to relate to each other and their work. How often do you return to a restaurant that has great food but lousy service? Nothing matters more to your brand than the way you serve customers or clients, and the way your team owns and shares the brand.

ACTION: *Can you identify all of the criteria that affect your customer's experience with you, then objectively grade your performance in each area? If you can, you have the basis for a very good service improvement program.*

_____

_____

_____

_____

_____

_____

_____

DAY TWO

A client recently shared that she had joined a 24-hour fitness center six months ago — and that was the last time she had been there. The problem? She needed to make an appointment with someone to run her through the machines and help her set initial weights and targets — but staff were only available when she wasn't. But here's the real problem. How does a 24-hour fitness center not realize that a new customer hasn't used her membership once in six months? Why have they not reached out to her to see how they can help her get started — before her membership expires and she just goes away?

ACTION: *How many of your customers aren't using many of the benefits they're paying for and could be enjoying? How many of them will just drift away if nothing changes? How can you intervene?*

_____

_____

_____

_____

_____

_____

_____

DAY THREE

All businesses operate on some basic assumptions about how they're doing. Sure - you have numbers to tell you how profitable the company is, or where sales are coming from. But how do you find out how *happy* your customers are with your service? You can take a passive approach, leaving surveys where customers can find them and fill them out, or adding a feedback page to your website. And you should. But the return is likely to be too small to tell you much. A proactive approach, where every transaction includes a question or rating designed to provide you with good feedback, can help you find and fix weaknesses, and will offer encouragement in those areas where you're performing well.

ACTION: *How can you build a system where you ask for — and get — feedback on every customer transaction, regardless of where and how it's conducted?*

DAY FOUR

A client once offered a challenging thought. When you buy a new vehicle, you don't expect the salesperson to take care of servicing it for you. That's what the service department is for. The salesperson devotes his or her time to checking in with you to make sure you're happy, letting you know about special deals, asking for referrals and developing new business. But in many other businesses, salespeople also have to service the clients they sell. This means they'll never reach their real sales potential, nor are they likely to deliver fabulous service, since their time is always divided and they make their money from sales. This challenges dozens of conventional business models, but it's worth considering.

ACTION: *What if your salespeople could sell, and your service people could serve? What would the net effect on profitability be? Higher sales? Higher customer retention?*

_____

_____

_____

_____

_____

_____

_____

DAY FIVE

It's easy to get so caught up in new business development, especially when times are tight, that you forget to love the ones you're with. Think about it: if you're working harder to woo new clients right now, competitors are working harder to woo your existing clients away from you. So while you work at effective ways to bring in new business, remember to lavish the same amount of time and attention on the clients you have now. If you've improved your range of products or services since they came on board, schedule some time to show them the benefits this is bringing them. Consider every client contact a new chance to cross-sell, to upsell — and most important, to re-sell them on the value of being a loyal client.

ACTION: *Where are the opportunities to show new options to longtime customers? What can you offer them to show your appreciation for their loyalty? A bundle that's a better deal? A new feature they don't have?*

_____

_____

_____

_____

_____

_____

_____

DAY ONE

Who do you trust when it comes to choosing a product or service? People you know probably top the list. But the second most-trusted source is online consumer ratings. Target is a great example of a retailer who lets buyers rate products and post their comments, good or bad, online. It may seem counter-intuitive, but the negative comments tend to lend more authenticity to all the ratings, so consumers trust them more — and that boosts online sales. That feedback also helps Target's buyers know which products are well-received.

ACTION: *How comfortable are you letting customers rate your products or services? If you're not, what does that tell you about your own perceptions of those products or services? Make them as good as they can be, then open yourself to ratings. The constant feedback will help you get better every day.*

DAY TWO

During a Youth Entrepreneur Success (YES) program, we were working with a group of young people who would be selling Pizza Hut pizza as their "company" product the next day. These middle school students all agreed that their product was better than Little Caesar's, which was being sold by a competing group. But when they stopped a group of college students (their target market) and asked their opinion, they all agreed instantly on Little Caesar's. Why? It cost less. These students, who were paying for their own pizza, valued price over taste. This came as a surprise to the YES participants, and was a big lesson for the young entrepreneurs: the only way to know what your customers want is to ask. Companies who guess do so at their own risk.

ACTION: *Do you know what your customers want, or are you making assumptions based on your own preferences or experience? How can you be sure?*

_____

_____

_____

_____

_____

_____

_____

DAY THREE

One benefit of the surge in online media is that it's never been easier
to find out what consumers think. Why does this matter? Because too
often, we make changes in the way we do business because it benefits the
organization. What if we could find out what our customers want, and
restructure around that? It's never been easier or less expensive. From
sending out e-mail inquiries to posting a feedback section on your website,
asking an online community or paying for an electronic survey, there are
dozens of ways to find out what customers think.

ACTION: *What information could help you serve customers better — and more
profitably? How can you find — or procure — that information online?*

_____

_____

_____

_____

_____

_____

_____

DAY FOUR

Here's a good example of how to use new media to your advantage. Papa John's once invited customers to create its next pizza offering. Using social media, the chain offered a slice of the profits, a lifetime supply of pizza and $1,000 in marketing dough to whoever concocted the winning recipe (the top three recipes were sold in its stores; the highest selling of the three took home the pies - er, prize.)

ACTION: *Think about your customers. Is there a way to tap their ideas to help you develop new products or services? And think about social media. Are you building a fan base you can activate for such an occasion?*

DAY FIVE

"What's wrong?" It's one of the most powerful questions in the English language. Now add three more words: "What's wrong with our service?" Most business leaders could easily learn what their companies are not doing well. But if they ask, they have to do something about the answer... and few look forward to that. So we seldom ask. Unfortunately, your competitors often know where you falter - and they're more than happy to exploit it for their own gain.

ACTION: *When was the last time you sat down with customers or your team (or even in front of a mirror) and asked where you could improve? Right now is a perfect time to ask the question — and to act on the answer.*

_____

_____

_____

_____

_____

_____

_____

DAY ONE

Too much of marketing revolves around what businesses want to say to consumers. But it's easy to forget this simple truth: just as you respond positively to a "good listener," so do customers. With the old "mass market" all but gone, opening the channels of direct, one-on-one communication in both directions has never been more important. How easy is it for your customers to let you know what they think? Do you make it easy? Just as importantly, do you see their comments - even their complaints - as the start of a conversation?

ACTION: *How easy is it for your customers to let you know what they think? Do you make it easy? Just as importantly, do you see their comments - even their complaints - as the start of a conversation?*

_____

_____

_____

_____

_____

_____

_____

_____

DAY TWO

One of the greatest temptations of the corner office is to assume that you know your customers. Business changes. People change. Tastes change. Habits change. And the rate of change in all areas is accelerating. So if you're basing your marketing decisions on assumptions grounded in the reality of five or ten years ago, there's a better-than-even chance that you're missing the mark. The only way to market well is to keep up with trends — shifts in buying patterns, changing demographics, absorption of new technology and so on. Otherwise, you run the risk of targeting the wrong people, marketing to them in ways that no longer reach them, or using messages that don't matter to them.

ACTION: *How do you and your company stay current on everything from shifting demographics to consumer trends and cultural shifts? How do you apply that knowledge to your marketing?*

_____

_____

_____

_____

_____

_____

_____

DAY THREE

When the Gatorade folks started to notice that athletes weren't emptying their bottles, they knew they had a problem. If the heaviest consumers of your product aren't downing the whole thing, what's happening at the more casual consumer level? The brand's chief marketing officer talked to some of their most loyal customers and found that they were getting burnt out and looking for something with the same punch, but lighter. The result was Gatorade Rain, the most successful brand extension in the product's history. It's a great reminder that customer defection, if detected early and responded to in a significant way, can lead to increased sales.

ACTION: *Would you notice if your customers weren't greeting your products with as much enthusiasm as usual? How can you know? How would you respond?*

_____

_____

_____

_____

_____

_____

_____

DAY FOUR

Companies often fail at the simple task of watching how customers use (or don't use) their products and services. Yet there's money to be made by paying attention. Just ask Heinz, whose observations of children using ketchup led them to develop a smaller bottle that's easier for kids to handle. The result? In homes where the EZ Squirt bottle is found, ketchup consumption rose by more than 10%. Keeping an eye on how your products or services are used can lead to new product ideas and better or more efficient ways to serve customers.

ACTION: *No matter your industry, are there ways you can monitor the way your products or services are consumed? What are they? How can you build a systematic process to track this important information?*

_____

_____

_____

_____

_____

_____

_____

_____

DAY FIVE

When was the last time you checked out a competitor's website? Now that it's incredibly easy to look in on your competition, it's astonishing how few companies actually do. So take a look. How is their site organized? Is it easy to navigate? User friendly? Intuitive? Does it include content that makes it easier for prospects to choose them? Is the layout clean and consistent with their brand and their other marketing messages? How fast does it come up using Google or Yahoo?

ACTION: *Now look at your own site. How do you compare in all those areas? Where do you excel, and where do you need work? Most important, how fast can you make the changes you need to make to be the leader?*

DAY ONE

In his terrific autobiography, *Open*, tennis great Andre Agassi talks about the importance of his racket stringer, "an old school, Old World, Czech artiste named Roman." Agassi elaborates on how a poorly strung racket can have a profound effect, costing the player the point that costs him the match that costs him income or even a career. It's a great reminder to do two things for your company. First, identify the little things that make the biggest difference to customers. Then, find the right people to put in charge of those things. If you find just one such thing today, you'll be ahead of your competitors.

ACTION: *When was the last time you gathered information from customers —and even non-customers — about the small things that matter most to them? How can you make this a recurring event? Then, how can you be sure the information is used to guide the choices you make?*

_____

_____

_____

_____

_____

_____

_____

DAY TWO

If you're old enough, you might remember Mitch Miller, the Columbia Records producer who was probably best known for his long-running TV schmaltz-fest, "Sing Along with Mitch." Miller was also head of Artists & Repertoire at the record label, where he knowingly dismissed rock and roll as nothing more than a passing fad. His experienced assessment? "It's not music, it's a disease." It's one more reminder, if any was needed, that it can be almost impossible to see past our own prejudices to catch a glimpse of what's coming next.

ACTION: *Is your "experience" in your industry blinding you to what lies ahead? How can you overcome this handicap to see the opportunities beyond it?*

_____

_____

_____

_____

_____

_____

_____

DAY THREE

There are reasons Coke is a market leader, and one of them is presentation. Coke was the first to introduce vending machines where customers could watch their bottle being selected and delivered. The company's Freestyle machine is actually a soda fountain, letting you choose from over 100 combinations. And in the U.S., Coke has long been widely available in glass bottles, while rival Pepsi has not. Branding happens on many fronts.

ACTION: *Can delivery become one your company uses? How?*

_____

_____

_____

_____

_____

_____

_____

_____

DAY FOUR

In a recent list of the top 100 ad campaigns of all time, just 3 were created after 1990, and most were from the 1970s and earlier. Why? Most modern advertising falls into one of two categories. Either it tries to entertain at the expense of selling, or it tries to sell but without being in any way engaging. Every one of the top 100 accomplished both: engaging the consumer and selling the product.

ACTION: *Does your marketing ring both bells? It should. What needs to change to make it so?*

_____

_____

_____

_____

_____

_____

_____

_____

DAY FIVE

Jay Conrad Levinson, author of *Guerilla Marketing*, defines advertising as "truth made fascinating." For an ad to work, it requires both elements. First, your product or service has to offer something unique that people want or need. That's the truth. Then you have to present that truth in a way that makes people laugh, that makes them curious, that makes them think — about you. That's the kind of advertising that actually works.

ACTION: *Does yours meet that test? If not, which aspect needs to be changed? Do you offer something special? Do you present it in an engaging, memorable way? If one of these is missing, how can you change that?*

_____

_____

_____

_____

_____

_____

_____

DAY ONE

People relate to people. Research shows that people also relate to marketing messages delivered by people, or featuring a human voice. When you look at or listen to your own marketing messages, do they have a voice of their own — a voice that humanizes your brand, and maybe even brings a little humor to the table? Not even an audible voice, either; a tone and choice of words that conveys a personality? That one simple change could easily double the effectiveness of your marketing.

ACTION: *What does your marketing voice sound like? If you don't have one now, to what kind of voice will your prospects respond?*

_____

_____

_____

_____

_____

_____

_____

_____

DAY TWO

Musician Jeff Lynne released an album which consisted entirely of new versions of hits he'd written for his old band, Electric Light Orchestra. Even though the originals were hugely popular, Lynne felt, after decades in the business, that he could do them better now. This poses a huge question for your business. Can you see that much progress in what you do? Are you continuing to improve year by year, so that you look at your old work and wish you could take another run at it? If not, you're either perfect or stuck. And nobody's perfect.

ACTION: *If you were starting from scratch today, what would you do differently? Can you do that now?*

_____

_____

_____

_____

_____

_____

_____

DAY THREE

Studies show that positive word of mouth is twice as effective as "traditional marketing." That's an important finding. Unfortunately, it's widely used as an excuse by companies who want to invest little or nothing in marketing, citing "word of mouth" as their best marketing tool. But word of mouth can be created, cultivated and encouraged.

ACTION: *If you could leverage your marketing to create something twice as effective, why wouldn't you? How does word of mouth happen in your industry? How can you insert your marketing into the process?*

_____

_____

_____

_____

_____

_____

_____

_____

DAY FOUR

When the financial crisis hit in 2008 and sales plummeted, most auto companies rolled out discounts and cash incentives, to little effect. Hyundai asked customers why they weren't buying, and heard the same answer over and over: fear. People were afraid to buy cars for fear they might lose their jobs and damage their credit ratings. That was the spark behind Hyundai Assurance, which guaranteed that buyers could return their cars if they lost their jobs within the first year of ownership. In the first month, Hyundai sales doubled, while all others continued their freefall. Two lessons, then. First, find the problem and make the solution your marketing pitch. Second, copy what works. Incredibly, no other automaker followed Hyundai's lead, even though they could all see the results. As a result, a lot of new Hyundai owners were created — folks who probably continue to buy the company's vehicles today.

ACTION: *Try thinking like Hyundai when it comes to solving your own problems. How can you come up with a solution that will not only fix the problem, but increase your sales?*

_____

_____

_____

_____

_____

_____

DAY FIVE

Next time you're at your local Redbox or movie theater, notice how similar — and similarly gruesome — all the covers are for horror movies. Now think back to two of the biggest and scariest: *The Exorcist* and *Alien*. The poster / cover for the former? A nighttime image of a man standing under a streetlight outside a home. The latter? A strange-looking egg beginning to crack, with light seeping through the fissure (and the admonition, "In space, no one can hear you scream.") No gore. No monsters. All suggestion. Here's the takeaway: trusting your target audience to have an imagination can help you produce marketing that engages them more.

ACTION: *How can you apply this strategy to your marketing in order to engage your audience more effectively? Their imagination is a powerful force.*

DAY ONE

Can a smartphone app make it easier to bring doughnuts to the office? Using DunkinRun.com, you can alert co-workers that you're making a doughnut run. They go to an online menu and add their choice to your list. You print the list and hand it to the cashier at Dunkin' Donuts, or simply show them the list on your phone — or submit the order online and have your doughnuts waiting at the store of your choice. The genius of this approach? It offers new convenience to customers while driving volume purchases.

ACTION: *How can you use technology to make it easier for customers to buy?*

_____

_____

_____

_____

_____

_____

_____

_____

_____

DAY TWO

Everyone knows that moms have found the internet to be a great resource for everything from health information to price comparisons. But how to use that information? Consider "cost per lead" advertising on relevant websites. Unlike their "cost per click" cousins, with CPL ads, you pay only for leads - for example, moms who sign up with their names and e-mail addresses. And you can narrow your focus to moms in your geographic market. But once you get them, engage them — whether you create a community to connect moms, send them regular coupons and special offers or provide them with valuable information.

ACTION: *Is your audience one that makes sense for CPL marketing? How narrowly can you define them, to ensure that you're truly paying for leads and not just names.*

_____

_____

_____

_____

_____

_____

_____

DAY THREE

It's no secret that newspapers are giving way to online news sources. And as that happens, the old ritual of reading the morning paper is quietly dying, replaced by web surfing. Online activity now sees a huge spike beginning at 6 a.m. each day as people wake up and plug in, checking e-mail, weather, traffic, school calendars, shopping and more. Texting takes off in the morning as well - morning messaging jumped 50% in a single year.

ACTION: *Consider this: if you want to be on consumers' minds as they start their day, how can you use the media they're using to engage them?*

DAY FOUR

A successful web presence takes two very different disciplines. It requires left-brain programming prowess to make sure everything is built correctly, well-organized and fully functional on a variety of browsers and devices (and to make sure the site gets found by search engines). It takes right brain creative skills to craft original content and develop a pleasing look and flow to the site that meshes with the brand. But the majority of sites lean one way or the other: pretty sites that are poorly organized, or unappealing sites that work well.

ACTION: *Does your site fall into one of these categories? If it does, you're probably missing opportunities. Take time to evaluate both sides of your site, and shore up where needed.*

_____

_____

_____

_____

_____

_____

_____

_____

DAY FIVE

The real beauty of today's internet for marketers, especially aspects like social media and blogs, is that anyone can take advantage of these effective and inexpensive tools to connect with customers. But too few businesses are truly seizing these golden opportunities. The universal reason: they take time. That vacuum creates an extraordinary opportunity for businesses willing to launch a blog, engage with fans through Facebook or create a conversation worth following on Twitter. Yes, it takes time. But like every worthwhile endeavor, that time is being invested in something that, done consistently and properly, can yield an enormous return.

ACTION: *Can you make time for more business? How will you begin?*

_____

_____

_____

_____

_____

_____

_____

_____

DAY ONE

Companies continue to invest heavily in SEO and SEM to drive web traffic. And that's all good. But what if your site doesn't offer visitors what they're looking for when they arrive? They won't stick around, and that investment gets wasted. So even as you optimize your site for search engines and plan a strategic PPC effort, be sure you know what it is your audience is really looking for in a site like yours. Their first priority is rarely to have you sell them something. So line your priorities up with theirs, and your investment will pay bigger dividends.

ACTION: *Do you know what your prospects are looking for online? Are they finding it on your site? If not, how can you fix it?*

_____

_____

_____

_____

_____

_____

_____

DAY TWO

As you consider how to make your website work harder, try making more demands of your visitors. Short commands and brief invitations are powerful tools. "Learn three secrets." "Watch the video." "Read more." "Download the whitepaper." "Listen here." As you add content to make your site more magnetic, make that content worthwhile — then make demands on your visitors. You may be surprised at the impact.

ACTION: *How many "calls to action" are on your site? How many invitations to take a next step, to download a resource, to watch a video or to sign up for something of value? What's one you could add right now?*

_____

_____

_____

_____

_____

_____

_____

_____

_____

DAY THREE

Captchas — those little boxes with hard-to-read words or combinations of letters you encounter online — are there to make sure you're a real human. What they often do is make sure you're frustrated, especially if you're on a mobile device, as more and more online traffic is. In fact, it's fair to say that captchas, far from helping capture business, often repel it.

ACTION: *Do your customers encounter captchas while online? Unless you have an incredibly good reason to incorporate them, don't. And if you have to use them, why not have a note explaining why?*

_____

_____

_____

_____

_____

_____

_____

_____

DAY FOUR

The digital world is a place where everything happens with blinding speed, right? Kind of. Some online moments live forever — and businesses don't spend enough time thinking about that. Here's an example. Write a blog post today. Five years from today, that post is still on your blog, still searchable — and still selling for you. Here's another. Someone endorses you on LinkedIn. That doesn't go away. So months or years from now, when a prospective client or employer is looking you over, that endorsement is as fresh as ever.

ACTION: *The lesson? Pay attention to the aspects of your digital world that are evergreen and actively engage in those areas.*

DAY FIVE

You'd never know it from the profits raked in by big pharma, but it's estimated that 20% of prescriptions go unfilled — and a whopping 70% of the rest go unused. Enter text messaging. Your doctor (or someone in the doctor's office) sends you a text message asking if you're taking your prescription or checking to see if it's having the desired effect.

ACTION: *If compliance is an issue for your customers, can you incorporate text messaging as a way to overcome it? Are there similar ways that text messaging can help you help customers? What are they?*

DAY ONE

An old rule of thumb that's been proven over and over again in print advertising appears to be equally true in the blogosphere: people like pictures, and they like pictures of people best. Some of the best-read consumer blogs being written today include photos of the writer engaged in the activities being written about. In any medium, people need to feel a connection.

ACTION: *Is a blog part of your online marketing effort? If so, consider posting pictures of real people that relate to your posts, and see what happens to readership. Same with social media posts.*

_____

_____

_____

_____

_____

_____

_____

_____

DAY TWO

You may buy milk by the gallon, but you don't consume it that way. A glass here, a bowl of cereal there...a little at a time. But consider e-mail. A lot of companies still send out infrequent e-mails that are as long as your arm. Who reads them? No one. It's too much. So why do they still do it? It's easier for them. They accumulate information for a month, then dump it all into one e-mail that no one reads. Instead, they should send out short items as they happen - and make sure they matter to the recipient.

ACTION: *If the point is to get read, begin with that end in mind. And **please** stop calling it a "newsletter"...the most sleep-inducing term on the planet. What information do your customers and prospects want from you?*

_____

_____

_____

_____

_____

_____

_____

DAY THREE

Yes, Facebook has more than a billion users, but the social medium may be most effective when the online world meets the real world. In Britain, fans of Heinz could nurse sick Facebook friends back to health by having a real can of Heinz soup sent to them. A laundry detergent cranked up the interactivity quotient as well, setting up a Facebook page where robots squirted various colors of stains on white shirts. Not only could fans control which colors the robots squirted, they also received the actual shirt, with stains cleaned away via the product.

ACTION: *If you're investing in social media, how can you break that wall between online and real life?*

DAY FOUR

If you place online ads using keywords, keep a couple things in mind. First, be as restrictive as possible. Since you're paying per impression or per click, even if it's a small amount for each, you want each to count. So target not just with the keywords themselves, but also confine results to your geographic market. This will help you avoid a lot of waste. And remember, this kind of advertising needs to have a very specific objective. For example, keyword advertising is a really ineffective way to build awareness. Target narrowly and sell something specific.

ACTION: *Do you know which keywords are best for your online ads? Are you testing different words, then adjusting based on the results?*

DAY FIVE

Most of the time, when a business decides to use social media, there's a "what," but no "why." For example, someone decides that the company needs a Facebook page, or a blog, or a Twitter account. And maybe they do. But why? Because everyone is doing it? Because someone in a seminar said so? How about this one: because creating a community of customers makes them more loyal, increases purchases and helps you improve what you sell and how you market it.

ACTION: *As you use social media, consider the results you hope to achieve. That will immediately refine which media you use and how you use them.*

DAY ONE

In all the frenzy over the latest entrant in the social media sweepstakes, don't forget that your website is often still a prospect's first impression of your business. And one of the easiest ways to make sure your page shows up high in search engine rankings is for lots of other sites to link to yours. That probably starts with figuring out new ways to have your site link to other sites. For example, if you have a "Clients" page, you can easily have each client's name link to their website. If you have other companies you work with on a regular basis, have links to those companies on your website. Once you do some of this, you're in a good position to ask them to place links to your site on theirs. And that pushes you closer to the top of the list.

ACTION: *Talk with clients, suppliers and other partners about ways to connect your websites for your mutual benefit. Start with a list.*

_____

_____

_____

_____

_____

_____

_____

DAY TWO

The baby boomers (born between 1946 and 1964) currently control the lion's share of the nation's wealth. And a majority of them text. Are those unrelated facts? They don't have to be. If you're targeting boomers, why not find ways to engage them with their mobile devices? Bank ads could include a code that you can text to be kept current on CD rates or loan specials. A restaurant can do the same on menus, urging diners to send a text to receive mobile updates about special offerings and events. Medical practices could encourage texters to sign up for reminders about annual check-ups or breaking health news.

ACTION: *If a big part of your market is made up of boomers, how can strategic mobile marketing help you stay in touch with them?*

DAY THREE

A lot of energy is spent on the right way to reach your audience with targeted web ads. But getting your ad in the right spot is only half the battle. The ad itself has to make its point in a persuasive way - in about three seconds. So think of digital ads as you would billboards. Make a compelling benefit statement in as few words as possible, then be sure the ad is crisp and easy to read. Just because you can have a cool animation created doesn't mean you should. Short, simple and strong equals click-throughs - the first step toward a sale.

ACTION: *How many clicks are your online ads generating? Can you experiment with different ads to see which perform best? Deploy, test, repeat.*

_____

_____

_____

_____

_____

_____

_____

DAY FOUR

When Ford re-entered the subcompact market with its Fiesta, it decided to use social media in a new way. The carmaker gave Fiestas to 100 consumers to use for six months — people in their 20s who were chosen for their very active presence on — and large networks in — social media. Over the next six months, Ford dispatched cars and drivers on missions ranging from charitable to romantic and even risky. The drivers then posted ongoing accounts (video and otherwise) of their Fiesta-fueled escapades on Twitter, Facebook, YouTube and Flickr. More important than the 6.5 million views on YouTube were the 50,000 requests for information about the Fiesta — and the 10,000 vehicles that drove off showroom floors in the first six days of sales.

ACTION: *In the social media frontier, the spoils are going to the pioneers. Are you one? What are three ways you could pull social media into the real life of your customers and your brand?*

DAY FIVE

Research shows that seniors (age 62 and up) who are online have higher intent to buy and twice the income of their offline counterparts — as well as twice the likelihood of a college education, a job and a spouse. If the target audience for your website includes seniors, make sure it shows. Use a clean layout, larger type (black on a white background is most readable) and larger links. Minimize choices, and shorten the path from arrival to purchase or contact. Most of all, be sure you make it easy for them to sign up for e-mail from you. And remember, this group is growing every day.

ACTION: *Are seniors a target audience for you? Does your web presence reflect this? What can you do better?*

DAY ONE

A lot of organizations - both businesses and not-for-profits - use events as a key element in their marketing / development strategy - and for good reason. Good events give you face time with people who are interested in what you offer. The downside is this: since most people are busier than ever, it's easy to skip an event if you've been there before and see no real reason to attend again. If you use events to drive interest in what you do, you have to outdo yourself with each one. People will return if you give them a strong reason; they'll pass if you don't.

ACTION: *What event do your prospects need? How can you add something new, or expand on something you presently do? How can you take advantage of online presentation tools to boost attendance or participation?*

_____

_____

_____

_____

_____

_____

_____

_____

DAY TWO

Everyone knows that some customers are more profitable than others. But what about those customers who might be profitable, but are simply awful people? Everyone dreads their calls and visits, their scowls and surliness, the unreasonable demands and perpetual dissatisfaction. Yes, they make you money, but at what cost to morale? And here's the difficult truth: they can't be satisfied, so no matter how you excel, they're still complaining about you (they complain about everyone). Firing a lousy customer can give morale a huge boost, and frees up resources to serve appreciative customers. And the one thing you won't have to worry about is the terminated customer telling anyone - the last thing they want to do is try to explain why they were asked to take their business elsewhere.

ACTION: *Are there customers you should fire today? Who are they? Who needs to do it?*

_____

_____

_____

_____

_____

_____

DAY THREE

Because consumer companies want lots of Facebook fans, they often "buy" them with contests or deals. But research shows that this kind of fan rarely engages with your brand. They take the deal to become a fan, then rarely, if ever, visit your page or interact with you on it. This is the polar opposite of what social media is designed to do, which is build genuine communities and open easy channels of real communication between you and your public. While you want your social media following to reach critical mass, it's better to have fewer followers who genuinely like you than a lot more who don't know you.

ACTION: *What's your social media plan? How can you give equal weight to fan / follower acquisition and engagement? How will you measure success?*

_____

_____

_____

_____

_____

_____

_____

_____

DAY FOUR

When Starbucks' Howard Schultz was considering a return as CEO after a 7-year absence - a return to a company that had begun to falter while he was away - he sought the advice of Michael Dell, who had been through a similar experience at Dell Computer. When Steve Jobs was relieved of management duties at Apple by his board in 1985, he spent some time with David Packard. You need someone you trust who has wisdom and experience you value — a person who can help you focus at those critical times.

ACTION: *When faced with a challenge or an opportunity, with whom do you consult? Who among your contacts might fill that role? Is it smarter to find someone outside your field?*

_____

_____

_____

_____

_____

_____

_____

DAY FIVE

There are at least two great things about the website Pixar created for *Monsters University*, the sequel to their hit, *Monsters, Inc.* The first is what a terrific promotional idea it was. But the second may get you rethinking your own marketing. For Pixar to create a faux college website and a recruiting video that are so dead-on speaks to how generic the real-life examples of both have become. The Pixar folks used every college marketing cliché in the book to perfect effect. You can still see the *Monsters University* site and video at monstersuniversity.com/edu/.

ACTION: *Think of your own industry and your own marketing. How easy would they be to spoof? The simpler it would be, the more likely it is that your marketing has become generic.*

DAY ONE

The first time you heard a car alarm go off, it got your attention, didn't it? What happens when you hear one now? If you're like most people, you just continue doing what you're doing. Unfortunately, that happens with companies, too. We learn to tune out the alarms and go about our business…until we go out of business because we ignored a warning sign. As fast as things change today, there's always an alarm you should be paying attention to, even if it's small and quiet right now.

ACTION: *What are the alarms that you may be tempted to ignore? How can you make sure you pay attention to them? Who else should be watching for them?*

_____

_____

_____

_____

_____

_____

_____

_____

DAY TWO

If you're fortunate enough to be the top competitor in your field or in your market, you get all the attention. The problem is, most of it isn't the kind you want. For a competitor to win market share, they have to attack you directly. If they get in front of a prospect, their only course of action is to compare themselves to you; to point out your weak spots and position themselves as being strong where you're vulnerable. If you're the market lion with the jackals snapping at your ankles, do two things today. First, remind customers and prospects that you're the leader for a reason. Reclaim the high ground and emphasize all the benefits you bring to the table as the top dog. And when one of the jackals distorts reality, call them out on it. In other words, cowboy up.

ACTION: *Your other task? Be ruthless in identifying your own weak spots, then shore them up. What's one you can start with today? What's one thing you can do to fix it?*

_____

_____

_____

_____

_____

_____

DAY THREE

If the deepening Hispanic population is part of your target market, remember that marketing to this audience means more than simply translating your English-language materials into Spanish. Keep in mind that colloquial Spanish is different from what you learned in high school. And remember that most American English expressions don't necessarily carry the same meaning when translated. For example, the famous "Got Milk?" translated exactly into Spanish, comes out, "Are you lactating?" Not quite the same thing.

ACTION: *If the Hispanic population is part of your target market, how are you reaching out to them now? How do you know if your (especially translated) communication is on-message?*

_____

_____

_____

_____

_____

_____

_____

DAY FOUR

Business owners or managers, whether new or experienced, often use friends and associates as an informal sounding board for everything from new products or new names to ad and logo designs. But unless those acquaintances are also marketing professionals (and maybe even then), you're likely to get a lot of diverse opinions without much (if any) consideration of your goals, competition and strategy. Review by committee almost never elevates a good idea, but nearly always dilutes one. Stay focused on your goals, trust your instincts and your creative partners, and your marketing will produce better results.

ACTION: *How do you make decisions on creative / marketing projects? Do you truly trust the marketing and design expertise of your partners in this area? If so, defer to their judgment rather than seeking non-expert opinions.*

DAY FIVE

One of the big problems with Groupon and similar online purveyors of discounts is that their frequent users rarely return to a business once they redeem their offers. They just move on to the next bargain. This refutes the basic premise that a person who samples your wares at half price will return at full price. But another, less obvious problem is this: those discount users are not customers of your business — they're customers of whoever supplied the discount. And without the relationship and communication channel, that business simply walks away. Relationships really do matter.

ACTION: *If you offer introductory discounts, consider the impact on future business. Are you undermining the value of what you sell when you discount the price? Are you generating profitable future business?*

_____

_____

_____

_____

_____

_____

_____

DAY ONE

Most of us watch TV to unwind. But as genuine reality TV deepens its hold on network schedules, your TV time can turn into a great prospecting tool. Just paying closer attention can tip you off to markets you may be missing. Here's an example. Watch HGTV and you'll notice that nearly all homebuyers, regardless of budget, seem to consider a home office a necessity. This should tell you that more people are operating businesses from their homes, are working from home (or at least taking work home), or have a side business they run from home in addition to their "regular" jobs. Are these people who could use what you sell? How would you let them know? And how can you relate all that at-home labor to the benefits you offer? Of course, that's just one example, but watching the way real people behave, even on TV, can turn up new markets for you

ACTION: *For the next couple weeks, watch TV differently. Pay attention to shows that feature real consumers or business people, and observe what matters to them. Are there opportunities in their behavior that can give you an edge?*

_____

_____

_____

_____

_____

_____

DAY TWO

If you were trying to win a new prospect, and they asked for references from existing clients or customers, are there any you'd be afraid to mention? If so, there's a good chance they hold the key to your future. Learning from failures is a critical part of success. So when you fail to deliver, seize the opportunity and ask what you can learn. Is there a way your lapse could have been avoided? What would you do differently now? The answers, if acted upon, will make you better.

ACTION: *Think of three former clients or customers for whom you could have done a better job. Have you changed your processes to reflect this? If not, what are two things you could do in the next month to prevent future mishaps?*

_____

_____

_____

_____

_____

_____

_____

DAY THREE

A pyramid chart describing the attributes of a stellar product applies equally to any company. The base is simply "performs as described," but as you ascend the pyramid, the other characteristics make all the difference: exceeds high expectations, feels like something was missing before they owned it, can't imagine not having it and so on.

ACTION: *What would have to change to push your company to the top of the pyramid, where brand is everything? Can you make those changes? When?*

_____

_____

_____

_____

_____

_____

_____

_____

_____

DAY FOUR

The better you get at what you do, the harder your job becomes. Think of hospitals. If you build a reputation for expertise in a particular area, you become the go-to destination for the most difficult and perplexing cases. Now look at your business. If you find yourself attracting increasingly challenging opportunities, it may be a sign that you're doing things right — that your brand is based on insight and expertise that your competitors lack. On the other hand, if you never see a tough case...

ACTION: *Do you find yourself handling increasingly complex or difficult situations for clients or customers? Are you capable of doing so? How can you communicate this? Are there case studies you can share online? What else?*

_____

_____

_____

_____

_____

_____

_____

_____

DAY FIVE

A magazine recently devoted several pages to the dozens of "beloved" restaurants in its city that have since closed their doors. Each received a glowing review, with the writer rhapsodizing about its virtues. And each is out of business. It's another reminder that having a great product or service is just the beginning. There's a tendency to assume that if we just do great work, we'll be successful. Not so. You have to remind people of your greatness over and over. Once you fall off the public's radar, you may be great, but you'll still be gone.

ACTION: *If you're doing great things, how do people know? Are they things that are in demand? Do you need to change what you offer or how you deliver it to stay relevant? How can you get people talking you up, especially on social media?*

_____

_____

_____

_____

_____

_____

_____

_____

DAY ONE

Recently someone was praising a competitor's publication. "I love the stories," they gushed. "I know," their companion replied, "I read it cover to cover." Did you catch that? It's the *stories*. It's always the stories. Pick your medium: Facebook, TV, print - stories sell. Stories create your brand's personality and make you easier to remember. So why do so few companies use stories as the foundation of their marketing? Probably because it's hard work. But then, everything that really moves the needle usually is.

ACTION: *Where are the stories in your business? Do they involve your customers? Your own team members? How can you tell your stories better?*

_____

_____

_____

_____

_____

_____

_____

_____

DAY TWO

On the TV series "House," Dr. Greg House excelled at two things: intentionally offending everyone in sight, and solving medical puzzles that baffle everyone else. He gets away with the former because of the latter. Customers will overlook a lot if you're ridiculously good at what you do — and if they can only get it from you. So get ridiculously good. Beyond that, and until you're that good, you absolutely have to do everything else right.

ACTION: *The truth is, you already know what you're not doing as well as you should. Identify it, then fix that first. Get good at everything — then get great.*

_____

_____

_____

_____

_____

_____

_____

_____

_____

DAY THREE

If you go to a conference with several speakers, you talk a lot about the ones who "wowed" you; you seldom even remember those who didn't. Public speaking can be a fantastic tool to help promote yourself and your business, but it only works if you're one of the memorable ones. If you speak - or if you want to - get serious about it. Have yourself videotaped, then watch every minute of it. You'll see and hear every bad habit you have. Give audiences a way to evaluate you, and read every one. Take a Dale Carnegie course. Watch TED talks and try to understand what makes the best speakers so good. If you work hard at being the one they remember, you won't have to work so hard at marketing.

ACTION: *From content to presentation, how can you make sure you're the one they remember? How can you learn from those who do it really well?*

_____

_____

_____

_____

_____

_____

_____

DAY FOUR

Want a truly embarrassing experience today? Go to your website, or grab one of your brochures or ads, and read it out loud. Not quietly, either - at a regular, conversational volume. Does it read the way people really talk? Or does it sound stiff and corporate? No one wants to read that. Jargon and buzzwords are overrated. If you want people to relate to your brand, make it personable. That means writing in a real voice, without overstuffed paragraphs and windy, cliché-ridden sentences. You can be professional and still be personal. Best of all, it's a fast, easy change to make — if you're willing to make it.

ACTION: *Start today with one page of your website — ideally your home page. Does it sound warm and engaging? Or does it sound like everyone else? Even with the need to satisfy SEO with the right words and phrases, you can do better.*

DAY FIVE

Why is networking so hard for so many people? Because few of us are truly wired for wading into a crowd of strangers and starting a conversation. But when someone approaches us, we do just fine. So how can you make that happen? By raising your visibility. Give a talk to a local organization. Write a column for a local paper or blog. Get interviewed by the local TV station or business publication. When you do, you become a familiar face — and people will come to you.

ACTION: *Today, write down three organizations you could join that make sense for your business. Choose one and join it. Then ask about serving on a committee or project. The more well-known you are, the easier networking will get.*

_____

_____

_____

_____

_____

_____

_____

DAY ONE

Too often, companies view their brand as a separate entity, to manage and shape, but the reality for most businesses is that your people are your brand. Obvious examples are Southwest Airlines or Zappos.com, but consider your own brand. Your people either reinforce it or negate it every day. No one is neutral. Even with an infinite marketing budget, you cannot create a brand unless you create a culture of true believers within your company.

ACTION: *Where in the interview process do you determine how well the candidate will enhance your brand? Would you turn away a really talented individual who wasn't a good fit for your brand?*

_____

_____

_____

_____

_____

_____

_____

_____

_____

DAY TWO

When Kraft Foods introduced DiGiorno Pizza, they knew what they were up against. They already had Tombstone and Jack's pizza lines, and research showed that people firmly believed that frozen pizza was vastly inferior to carry out and delivery (CO/D). Kraft made at least three smart moves with DiGiorno. First, it started with a better product than previous contenders. Next, it had a smart brand statement: "It's not delivery, it's DiGiorno's," with equally smart advertising. Finally, it gave away tons of samples to let customers see for themselves. Not only did sales and especially repeat purchases exceed forecasts, but they came at the expense of CO/D brands — a much bigger market than frozen pizza.

ACTION: *Is there a way you could adapt this model to your own product or service offerings? Can you change the conversation by changing the comparison? How can people sample what you offer?*

_____

_____

_____

_____

_____

_____

_____

DAY THREE

If a prospect walks in the door, calls on the phone or goes to your website and is ready to buy, you don't need a crack sales team to close the deal. What would put the prospect in the mood to buy from you? A brand that's different from - and better than - your competitors'. It's a crucial point that's often lost in all the talk about branding. If you take the time to create a truly unique position in your market, then invest the time to make sure your people can communicate that difference easily and consistently, a lot of sales will follow.

ACTION: *Walk around and ask your employees what makes you different. Do they all have the same answer? Is it the right answer? Would it persuade a prospect to become a customer? If not, there's your next project.*

_____

_____

_____

_____

_____

_____

_____

DAY FOUR

Most companies struggle to clearly define what makes them unique among — and better than — their competition. But without that differentiation, marketing becomes very expensive — and not so effective. So what happens if you simply can't find anything that separates you from the pack? Short of throwing in the towel and accepting whatever crumbs fall your way, your best bet is to go back to the drawing board - to look for a new product to create, a new service to offer or a new way of doing things that will fill a need (even if people don't yet know they need it - see Apple for lots of examples). Distinction that matters is the key to a brand that makes marketing easier.

ACTION: *How much time are you willing to devote to finding new products or services, or new delivery models that will make you stand out? What resources will you commit to this effort? You get what you pay for, in time and money.*

_____

_____

_____

_____

_____

_____

_____

DAY FIVE

Years ago, the late soul crooner Sam Cooke offered fellow singer Bobby Womack some advice that applies to brands as well as songs. Cooke said that if people could sing along with a song, it stood a much better chance of becoming a hit. A song with a lot of vocal acrobatics might be appreciated, Cooke noted, but was less likely to become a classic. The same is true with your brand. If people can relate to everything about your company — your products, your people, your marketing — on an instinctive, personal level, your brand will run very deep with those folks, as they do with their favorite sports team. Make it too complicated, and while people may admire you, they won't love you. And you want people to love your brand.

ACTION: *How can you both simplify your brand and make it run deeper with consumers? What's one way in which people relate emotionally to what you offer? How can you tap into that?*

_____

_____

_____

_____

_____

_____

_____

DAY ONE

Building a brand is really hard. In a world where competitors all promise (and may even deliver) the same exact things, separating yourself can seem impossible. Which brings us to Superman and Batman. Reasonable people look at Superman and understand that they can never do what he does. He's from another planet, and he has superpowers. But Batman is a different story. He's just a guy. Sure, he had a lot of money. But his ability to do what he does is based on nothing but relentless hard work and training. You can look at branding either way: impossible, or just incredibly hard.

ACTION: *Will you settle for being "one of many," or are you willing to work relentlessly to be different – and heroic?*

DAY TWO

Take a look at the new releases in a local bookstore (we still have a few, don't we?). Which is set in larger type: the title or the author's name? If it's the latter, that author is a strong brand, and the publisher knows that the name (J.K. Rowling, Stephen King) will sell more books than any title they can imagine. The lesson here is the importance of branding. When you enjoy a strong brand, you don't have to sell specific products or services so hard; people want what you have, and want to associate themselves with your brand. Think Apple, Under Armour, etc. And one way to get people to covet your brand is to court and promote the influencers who use you now.

ACTION: *Who among your customers is someone with influence among your prospects? How can you court those people and persuade them to be advocates and enthusiasts for your brand? A special event? Special status? What else?*

_____

_____

_____

_____

_____

_____

_____

DAY THREE

When singer Andy Williams died, every news story began with the same thing: a clip from the hit song "Moon River," which Audrey Hepburn sang in the film *Breakfast at Tiffany's*. This, in spite of the fact that Williams scored 27 other Top 40 hits, including two songs from bigger movies (*Love Story* and *The Godfather*), had a popular TV show and a long run of Christmas TV specials. In fact, "Moon River" doesn't even appear in Williams' Billboard listing; it appears under composer Henry Mancini's name. Regardless, the song continues to define the singer. There's a lesson here about your brand. The single most powerful factor that affects your brand is public perception. It's your job to help them perceive the right things.

ACTION: *Does your marketing reflect the brand attributes you want consumers to embrace? If not, you're limiting your brand.*

_____

_____

_____

_____

_____

_____

_____

DAY FOUR

Brazil has always evoked the idea of exotic beauty. But in 1987, the seven J. Sisters made the trip from their family beauty salon near the beaches of Espirito Santo to open a shop on 57th Street in the Big Apple. They introduced the rigorous Brazilian approach to manicures and pedicures, and their business blossomed. But their big moment came in 1994, when they began offering the "Brazilian bikini wax." The norm for Brazilian women and their micro-bikinis, it was foreign to these more modest shores — until Sarah Jessica Parker's character on "Sex and the City" got one and demand exploded. Today, adding the word "Brazilian" to any beauty product or procedure opens the door to charging a premium price.

ACTION: *In your own industry, what words suggest a premium product or service? If the answer is "none," what descriptors can you borrow from an industry other than your own to position your most profitable offerings as worth a premium price?*

_____

_____

_____

_____

_____

_____

DAY FIVE

Look at the curriculum for most Marketing MBA programs, and they're loaded with math classes. Which is interesting, because a failure to grow market share is almost never a math problem. It's almost always a branding issue — a failure to convince prospects that you're the best choice, or to compel them to make the purchase. The math matters, but in the end, it all comes down to presenting a unique brand in an appealing way that makes people want to act. And that's the bottom line.

ACTION: *Are you so focused on marketing ROI that you've lost track of marketing's foremost goal — to construct a brand that generates sales? If you focus on the brand, the math takes care of itself.*

_____

_____

_____

_____

_____

_____

_____

_____

DAY ONE

For several years running, GoDaddy tried to inject shock value into its Superbowl commercial. Its 2013 spot was no exception, with its supermodel-on-supergeek action. The big question is whether it works. Here's how to find out. If you were going to buy a domain name for a website, where would you start? If GoDaddy has become the Google of domain name sellers, then their annual Superbowl shocker paid off. The lesson isn't that you need to shock buyers. It's that you need to start a conversation about your brand.

ACTION: *Does your marketing get anyone talking? If not, it's failing a critical test, and leaving an enormous opportunity on the table. If you wanted your marketing to create some buzz, how would it change what you're doing?*

_____

_____

_____

_____

_____

_____

_____

DAY TWO

Time and again, companies learn that what customers often value most is consistency. They want to know that every time they call, visit or otherwise engage with you, the experience will be dependably, reliably the same…in a good way. Think about your favorite brand, especially one that involves food or drink. You want this Pepsi (or Coke, or Starbucks, or Dogfish Head 90-Minute IPA) to taste exactly as good as the last one. The good news? Consistency can be created and reinforced with good systems for training, reinforcing and measuring. And that's the best marketing investment a company can make.

ACTION: *How do you train to your brand? What systems are in place to ensure a consistent brand experience? Where do you need to improve?*

_____

_____

_____

_____

_____

_____

_____

DAY THREE

How did "Downton Abbey," a British drama on PBS, become one of the most watched shows on television, with its heartrending Season 3 finale beating every broadcast and cable show in its time slot? By understanding that if you craft a compelling story, beautifully written and played to perfection, you'll draw the audience to you — even without the marketing budget of bigger competitors. Marketing your brand is no different. Tell a powerful story in a rich, engaging way, and people will watch to see what you do next.

ACTION: *How can you take what PBS did on their television show and apply it to your own marketing strategies? Do you have a moving story you can tell? Write a one-paragraph version today. Now, how can you tell it in all media?*

_____

_____

_____

_____

_____

_____

_____

_____

DAY FOUR

Looking for a way to get a little brand recognition? Consider apparel. We're not talking about a golf shirt with your logo, here. Think of some truly fun or clever t-shirt your target audience would really want to wear. Whether your best prospects are twenty-somethings, baby boomers or even babies, if you can develop a "line" of apparel that people will really like, then attach your brand to it, your identity will be worn all over the place. The gold standard? When your gear is so popular that people will pay you to wear it.

ACTION: *Spend a couple lunch hours brainstorming apparel ideas that might appeal to your audience and cast a "cool" halo over your brand. What would it take to get the best ones designed and into the hands of people who'll wear them? And remember, design matters.*

_____

_____

_____

_____

_____

_____

_____

DAY FIVE

Want a humbling experience? Try this one. Go to one of your competitors' websites and read what it says about them on their home page. Now go to another competitor's site and do the same. Repeat this a couple more times. Is there anything those sites say that sounds different than what you'd say about your company? Now go to your own site. Does it say anything different? If not, you're not really branding — you're blending in.

ACTION: *In what ways is your website is just like your competitors'? What would it take to change that? When can you start?*

_____

_____

_____

_____

_____

_____

_____

_____

_____

DAY ONE

One of the most effective marketing approaches — assuming that what you offer or the way you offer it is up to the task — is to make your brand aspirational. Make doing business with you, using your services or your products, something that people strive for. "The Car That Car Lovers Love." "For Serious Athletes Only." "First Choice of Foodies Everywhere." "Where Smart Moms Shop." If you want to be the brand of choice, position yourself that way.

ACTION: *What traits can you assign to the products or services you offer — or to your company? Now incorporate the most powerful into your marketing messages, and see what happens.*

_____

_____

_____

_____

_____

_____

_____

DAY TWO

Your brand is the aggregation of what people think and feel about your company and what you sell. And some of those people are *your* people. When was the last time you asked your own team what they think your brand is? Here's why it matters. If the people who are actually delivering the products or services aren't aligned with your vision for the brand, they can't deliver on it. Branding works best from the inside out.

ACTION: *Especially if you've never asked, survey your entire team and ask them to tell you what they think your brand is — what you stand for and what makes you unique. Starting from there, begin relentlessly selling your vision of the brand back to them. Then stand back and see who gets it.*

_____

_____

_____

_____

_____

_____

_____

_____

DAY THREE

People tend to see the doctor less often when they're young, and more often as they get older. But we do just the opposite with brands. When a company is young, there's often a lot of attention paid to brand awareness and perception, competition, market trends and more. But as a company matures, management seldom does the same diagnostic work, assuming that they know exactly who they are in the minds of consumers and where they are in the marketplace. And that can lead to a lot of inefficient marketing.

ACTION: *If it's been awhile, consider a brand diagnostic that will give you a true "head to toe" look at your business and your brand? Write it down. It's the best way to keep your brand and your bottom line healthy.*

_____

_____

_____

_____

_____

_____

_____

_____

DAY FOUR

If you think of a brand as a company's personality, then having a strong one helps drive profits in two ways. First, it attracts customers who are drawn to your brand qualities or persona. The other is that it keeps your marketing focused on reinforcing those qualities. That keeps marketing on-message, which makes it more effective

ACTION: *Can you describe your brand's personality? Is it the one you intended — one that draws customers in? Write a description of your brand using "personality" words, and see where it takes you. You might be surprised.*

_____

_____

_____

_____

_____

_____

_____

_____

DAY FIVE

It's been called a hundred different things, but every business needs one. It's the single statement that tells people why you're a better choice than your competitors. It singles you out and makes you the go-to source for what you do. And you should never stop working on it. This single statement — let's call it your brand position — can always be a little clearer, a little tighter or pack a little more punch. And it should change as you do. So keep polishing it until it gleams.

ACTION: *Do you have a statement of your brand position? Is it striking? Bold? Relevant? How can you improve it? Does your team know it?*

_____

_____

_____

_____

_____

_____

_____

_____

_____

DAY ONE

It's no secret that companies are reconfiguring customer service so it makes sense for them first, and the consumer second (if at all). That's why it's so hard to find a phone number for customer service on many websites — they don't want your call. But consider the Geek Squad. Recognizing the desire so many of us have to deal with an actual person, they built a company of them — people who would come to your home or business. This admittedly retro idea was so well-received that Best Buy bought the company.

ACTION: *Now look at your own industry. Is there some aspect of customer or client service that's vanishing — something you could find a profitable way to reintroduce?*

_____

_____

_____

_____

_____

_____

_____

_____

DAY TWO

How many competitors do you have? Think about all of them — local, regional, national and online rivals, all courting the same customers as you. Now forget them, and think about that customer. In almost every category, she's overwhelmed by more choices than ever before. It's your job to offer relief. Make the choice so obvious that it's easy.

ACTION: *Ask your customer what matters most, or bugs her most, or is missing — then fix it and build your brand on it. It's both extremely simple and incredibly difficult — but it succeeds every time. Start today. Just ask.*

_____

_____

_____

_____

_____

_____

_____

_____

DAY THREE

The next time you're tempted to use the same overused words and phrases in your marketing — service and quality and all the rest — get specific instead. Give examples and facts and numbers that show what you do and how much better it is than the competition. If you're a CPA firm, and your clients get audited less, say so — and say how much less. Stop generalizing; no one believes it. Sales are in the details.

ACTION: *What are some specific claims you can make that offer a clear benefit to your customer? Even if your competitors could make them, they're probably not. Be the first. Specificity sells.*

_____

_____

_____

_____

_____

_____

_____

_____

_____

DAY FOUR

The vast, overwhelming majority of marketing messages are infected with the same deadly virus. They're not designed to sell. Everything from the choice of colors to typefaces (and type size) to images and even paper should be chosen based on what you're selling and to whom. Yet most marketing falls into the two extremes: no thought given to design at all, or a focus on aesthetics over sales. Every design choice matters. Bad (or thoughtless) design is the bad breath of marketing — it reliably repels interested parties.

ACTION: *Are the design choices behind your marketing based on sound sales principles or someone's personal preferences? How can you tell? If refining this would impact sales, would you do it? Because it will.*

_____

_____

_____

_____

_____

_____

_____

DAY FIVE

These days, providing your customers with online access is just a cost of doing business, not an option. But here's the dilemma. As personal interactions (more expensive, to be sure) are replaced by online transactions (more cost-effective for you, more convenient for the customer), you have to find new ways to build a relationship with your customers — the kind of relationship that translates into repeat business, higher utilization and greater loyalty. As you continue the online migration, few issues will be bigger.

ACTION: *How are you adapting what you do to build relationships with your online customers? How do you know if they're happy? How can you find out what they need?*

_____

_____

_____

_____

_____

_____

_____

_____

DAY ONE

Ever wonder why a mission statement or vision statement so rarely generates real enthusiasm? It's because they all rely on the same generic words and phrases that suck the life out of marketing — words like best, excellence and so on that are so vague as to be unactionable. Like your marketing messages, your mission and vision statement should sell. There should be a real call to action, much as Pepsi once had when their entire mission statement was simply, "Beat Coke." Read their current mission statement and see which you prefer.

ACTION: *Read your mission statement. Would anyone get excited over it? Would it inspire a new hire? If you want a team filled with missionary zeal, give them a mission worth being excited over.*

_____

_____

_____

_____

_____

_____

_____

DAY TWO

Visit a Chick-Fil-A location, and whether you use the drive-thru or go inside, you're sure to hear someone respond to you with the phrase, "It's my pleasure," almost always delivered with a sincere smile. It may seem insignificant, but it isn't. It sends a clear signal that theirs is a customer-focused business — that you matter to them, and that they're pleased to be able to serve you. Of course, it takes more than a phrase to deliver great service, from smart hiring to consistent training and reinforcement. But delivered with a smile, it's the touchstone of their customer experience.

ACTION: *What's your signal to customers that their experience is your priority? What should it be? What needs to happen to bring that about?*

DAY THREE

In his wonderful memoir, *Life Itself*, film critic Roger Ebert credits a colleague, Bill Lyon, with the most useful advice he was ever given as a journalist: to stop waiting for inspiration and start writing, and to keep writing until the end. The idea, in Ebert's words, was to "spend less time not writing." This is incredibly powerful for marketers, too. No one ever comes up with a big idea by staring at a blank screen or sheet of paper. You have to start — then your brain engages, and one thing leads to another.

ACTION: *Whether you're working on marketing messages, product ideas or ways to improve service, just start — and keep going.*

DAY FOUR

We know that a smile means a person is happy. But research shows that smiling actually *makes* you happy. In other words, the more you smile, the happier you'll feel. This is great news for business. If you can persuade your front line, customer contact people to smile more, two things will happen. The first is that you'll have a happier team. The second is that a lot of your customers will smile back. This will make them feel happier, and they'll associate that good feeling with doing business with you.

ACTION: *Begin a crusade to get every team member to smile at every customer, every time. It's an easy change you can make today. And remember to have people smile while they talk with customers on the phone, too — people can hear a smile.*

DAY FIVE

There's a critical step at the core of effective marketing, yet it's often overlooked. It's finding the real answer to a seemingly simple question: what does your company — or the products and services it provides — actually do for customers? It's overlooked because the answer seems obvious. It's crucial because it really isn't as obvious as it seems. A paint manufacturer understands that it isn't in the business of making wall coatings; it makes it possible for customers to transform their surroundings and their moods. Richard Branson of Virgin Airlines understood that he was in the entertainment business, not the travel business.

ACTION: *Consider it carefully and answer it differently: what do you do?*

_____

_____

_____

_____

_____

_____

_____

_____

DAY ONE

In the sports world, as demonstrated in books like *Moneyball* and films like *Draft Day*, success in recruiting often means seeing what no one else sees. The same is true for your company. If you're not looking at your industry and your customers and asking yourself what everyone is missing, you'll never have the insights that can fuel innovation and push you out ahead of your competitors.

ACTION: *Take a look around today at your company, your competition and your industry and ask the question: what's everybody missing? Where's the money in the answer?*

_____

_____

_____

_____

_____

_____

_____

_____

DAY TWO

There are beloved, award-winning advertising campaigns — Coke's sunny "I'd like to teach the world to sing," Taco Bell's chihuahua — that earned rave reviews, but didn't really have the desired impact on sales. Meanwhile, those hammy TV spots where a gregarious spokesperson hawks the latest cleaning product or gadget? They sell millions of units. In our desire to make our marketing clever or edgy or memorable in some other way, it's easy to lose sight of the fact that marketing has just one goal: to sell something. Your marketing can be catchy and unique — it has to be, to break through the clutter — but if it doesn't sell, it's a waste of time and money, both of which are finite commodities.

ACTION: *How can your marketing be memorable **and** sell harder?*

_____

_____

_____

_____

_____

_____

_____

_____

DAY THREE

Let's say you're a bank or a credit union. Suppose someone moves into your market — maybe a highly paid executive taking over the top job at a local company. That executive will need a lot of banking services. What do they need to know to choose you over a competitor? And how are you making sure that they — and all good prospects — have that information at their fingertips? Regardless of your business, you have to help people know what makes you the best choice.

ACTION: *How do you position your competitive advantages so hot prospects will see them? What's one thing you can do today to improve in this critical area? (You do have competitive advantages to offer, right?)*

_____

_____

_____

_____

_____

_____

_____

_____

DAY FOUR

True story. A company provided its sales team with a gorgeous (and expensive) collateral package that included an elaborate folder with materials of all kinds to fit into various slots, slits and pockets. It was beautiful. Months later, the packets were still sitting in boxes instead of being given out to prospects. Why? The salespeople knew that it was too much information. Prospects would simply be overwhelmed, and those expensive packets would end up in the trash. If marketing had met with sales ahead of time to talk about what they really needed, they would have saved time and money, and the sales people would have had practical tools they could use to land new business.

ACTION: *Before you provide your sales team with materials to support what they do, ask them what they need. Better yet, accompany them on sales calls for a day or two. You'll use your resources more wisely and productively.*

DAY FIVE

Plenty of companies use incentives to lure new customers. Let's flip that around for a minute. What incentive would make *your* good customers defect to your competition? Does that reveal a weakness you can work on — an opportunity to fortify your position? And as you think about incentives, consider what you could offer existing customers that could make them tamper-proof.

ACTION: *What incentive— a new feature, smoother delivery, an upgrade, bundle pricing — could fortify your position with your existing customers and make them more loyal? How hard would it be to execute?*

DAY ONE

A TED Talk by educator Rita Pierson points out two things that should be obvious. Kids learn more from teachers they like. And they like the teachers who like them. Same goes for customers. They stick around when they feel the love, and they drift away when they don't. Instead of working so hard to get likes on Facebook, spend some time making sure that you and your team like your customers — and that your customers *feel* liked. Here's a helpful hint: that's easier if you like your team.

ACTION: *Do your customer service people like customers? Or do they roll their eyes and complain about them? You may need to reshuffle your team a little.*

_____

_____

_____

_____

_____

_____

_____

_____

DAY TWO

It's so simple an idea that it's easy to overlook. Most of the customers or clients you win came from a competitor of yours. This means that you have a rare opportunity to ask why? Why did they switch? How long did the relationship last? Why leave now? The answers can do more than give you a sense of where your competition is vulnerable; they can help you understand what matters to your customers, so you can keep them longer.

ACTION: *How hard would it be for you to gather this important data from new customers? How can you build this into a systematic process of gathering and reviewing that gives you new insights into customer retention?*

_____

_____

_____

_____

_____

_____

_____

_____

_____

DAY THREE

As marketers, we spend so much time trying to generate leads that we sometimes overlook what happens when a prospect finally becomes a customer. Do you have a system in place to ensure that every new customer gets a call — not an e-mail, but a phone call — a day or two after that first transaction, just to make sure everything met the expectations you've created? You should, because it accomplishes two things. First, it makes the new customer feel more welcome and begins that important process of building loyalty. Second, it lets you know right away if the way you bring new customers onboard isn't what it should be — and gives you a chance to repair any damage that was done if the transaction didn't go well.

ACTION: *What do you do to make new customers feel welcome — and to show them that you take their business personally? When does this contact stop? Why?*

_____

_____

_____

_____

_____

_____

_____

DAY FOUR

If your company is like the majority of businesses, you may be guilty of taking your customers for granted. Oh sure…they get a statement every month, or an e-mail…but you've long since stopped trying to sell them on your brand. You know who hasn't stopped? Your competition. Just like you, they're devoting most of their marketing resources to reach new prospects, leaving their existing customers vulnerable to smooth-talking marketers who promise bigger, better or faster for less.

ACTION: *Don't let your customers be tempted to leave. Make sure your marketing plan includes a plan to keep them happy. What are the first three steps?*

_____

_____

_____

_____

_____

_____

_____

_____

DAY FIVE

A recent visit to a website suggested that the company "specialized" in nearly thirty different industries. That's not specialization. In fact, it's the exact opposite — it's a company that dabbles, doing projects in every market segment but never truly digging deep enough to own any individual niche. True specialization is the engine that drives powerful brands. You stake out a specific area, and master it so thoroughly that you become the "go to" company for anyone needing assistance in that area. Of course, it's perfectly fine to handle a broad range of clients. But if you're going to call yourself a specialist, have a real specialty.

ACTION: *What is your specialty — the thing you do better and more expertly than anyone else? If you don't have one, what specialty could you develop?*

THANK YOU

The contents of this book have taken shape over nearly ten years, and a few individuals deserve special thanks for playing a part in that process. I'm grateful to Tonja Sunderhaus, who was present at the inception of The Marketing Minute and who sent it out into the world for years; to all those who offered feedback, advice and the occasional correction; to Morgan Vellinger, who took on the daunting task of sifting through hundreds of "Minutes" to help organize them into some semblance of order; to Gary Clark of Clark & Riggs, our printing partner for many years, for his guidance and advice; to Blair Enns for giving this the final push it needed; to Lisa Howie for ceaseless encouragement; and to Michael Howie, who is more inspiring than he knows.

NEED MORE?

Visit themarketingminute.com to sign up for new content delivered directly to your inbox.